Pira Sudham
Tales of Thailand

ISBN 974-89628-5-7

Copyright © by **Pira Sudham**

The Fifth Cycle Edition

Published in 2002

Shire Asia Publishers
GPO 1534, Bangkok 10501, THAILAND
Fax: 044-686040, 044-686093
International Fax: 66 44 686040, 66 44 686093
E-mail: shireasia@yahoo.com

UK Representative
Rothershire
E-mail: rothershire@yahoo.com.uk

Books by Pira Sudham
Monsoon Country
The Force of Karma
People of Esarn

"It is not only a pursuit of knowledge but also the process of reasoning and thinking and opinion forming to rebuild a mind that has been maimed during the formative years by an age-old educational system so as to become a thinking person. You and I have been subjected to authoritative teaching and rote learning meant to induce obedience, subservience and mindlessness. We are supposed to become unthinking, silent and submissive so as to be governable, exploitable and harmless. We are not supposed to have inquiring minds and critical thinking, to be opinionated, forthright and opposing the authorities in any way. But like a pregnant woman safeguarding the foetus in the womb, I have to take care of the seed in my head until it could be germinated and evolve. At present I have to keep the effort to think profoundly and to write well hidden so that in the meantime the deprived mind can be developed into a stronger and more capable thinking tool. Meanwhile a consuming force is relentlessly driving me to deliver an end result, a book, on an agenda that belongs to destiny rather than my own design."
-Prem Surin in *Monsoon Country* (Mahanaga Edition)

Gustav Erne

A Journey in hidden Thailand

When we hear about Thailand today, we are told mostly about the collapse of financial institutions, about hundreds of unoccupied office towers and condominiums and a myriad of unfinished building sites, which expose their steel reinforcements to the elements. We read about the closure of many factories and the laid-off workers' demonstrations to claim severance payments, with which employers were reluctant to part, following the economic crisis that occurred in July 1997. Again and again we go through daily the mammoth traffic jams in highly polluted Bangkok. Meanwhile, potential visitors have been exposed to promotional materials that draw tourists to Bangkok, Pattaya, Samui and Puket. Occasionally we might see a scandalous documentary on sex-tourism, child trade and prostitution. But we hear very little about the parched plains of Esarn in the northeast of Thailand, or about the plight of the Esarn people, who speak Lao rather than Thai.

Author Pira Sudham has become the international voice of these forgotten people. In Esarn, the questions of grinding poverty, exploitation by unscrupulous merchants, factory owners and government agencies, destruction of the ecology, greed and ignorance are inextricably linked. Pira Sudham has written one story called *The Gunman* in which he narrates how professional gunmen are hired to murder a schoolteacher who is idealistic and courageous enough to try to protect a dwindling forest reserve, teaching the village children that they are entitled to a better deal. In another story, *The Impersonator,* he exposes the scandalous selling of children into prostitution, a sordid reality that required a special writing skill to make it palatable.

As Pira Sudham shows, education for literacy and democracy is the key to overcoming this vile exploitation. But there is of course education and education. If education consists of nothing more than rote learning, which reinforces mindlessness, unthinking nationalism, subservience and absolute obedience to local leaders and Bangkok authorities, it is worse than useless. But educators who encourage the children to question the authorities on various social issues including corruption and the selling of the young into prostitution and child labour in Bangkok's factories are likely to be seen as a threat. Ten Esarn schoolteachers have in fact been murdered.

As researchers, we humanists are morally useless if we focus only on the linguistics and the aesthetics of minority languages and traditional minority cultures. The larger issues are the politics of education, of literacy for the neglected and impoverished people, the human rights of the suppressed ethnics.

Following the heavy fighting with the insurgents in various parts of Esarn in the 1970s, the authorities have set up 'forced listening' in Esarn villages by broadcasting, through loudspeakers installed on tall steel posts, official government news and messages by Radio Thailand based in Bangkok. As Pira Sudham explains, this daily enforced listening has regrettable consequences for the cultural literacy and ethnic identity of the Esarn people. Broadcasts made in the Thai language are aimed at making the Lao-speaking Esarn people feel that they are 'Thai' and should be loyal to the Thai government rather than foment insurgencies and demand separatism. The monopoly of Radio Thailand has succeeded in diminishing the opportunities of the Esarn people to listen to broadcasts by local radio stations in the Lao language, which they previously enjoyed. Less and less frequently the Esarn people hear Esarn songs and music on the radio, and eventually they may be induced to forget their traditional culture and even their Lao language.

When one travels through Esarn, it is not difficult to see the steel posts strategically installed in villages to hold the loudspeakers. The enforced listening would not come as a surprise in a country that is ruled by despots, but in modern Thailand it is really a remarkable occurrence. In the Western democracies if governments tried to impose such a blatant broadcast, the noise pollution alone would create an overwhelming outcry. But in Esarn the voiceless people are afraid to speak up against the authorities.

It is clear that there are inextricable links between literacy, education, democracy and human rights. This could not be clearer than the case of the Esarn people. It is in this context that the author would like to take readers on a journey to the hinterland of Thailand:

"I look at my life in this way: If I had not left my village at all, I would have become just another peasant with a horde of children, going through the vicious circle of rural life in a poor village in Esarn. If ignorance is blissful, I could have been a happier person. Like most villagers, I would believe that going through years of drought, scarcity and disease without medical treatment, without any relief, in a forlorn Esarn village is my destiny, my fate or *karma* for what I committed in my previous life. So in this life, I am to suffer for the deeds done. The acceptance of one's fate would make suffering in this life tolerable. It was in England from 1975 onward when I began leading a life of a writer that I had to look deep into my heart and soul for a cure, a way to repair my maimed mind. It became obvious to me then that when young, I was gagged and blindfolded by the despotic regimes under which I lived for over fifteen years beginning in 1958 when military rule under Field Marshal Sarit Dhanarat took off. Worse still, it was rote learning, which is much alive and well in Thailand today, particularly in rural schools that became a mind-maiming apparatus. I was taught and trained to become utterly obedient, subservient, unthinking, fearing the authorities.

"James Joyce says in *A Portrait of the Artist as a Young Man* that when a child is born in Catholic Ireland, nets are flung to catch his soul. In my society, it is not the nets but the instrument to nip the mind in the bud or to stunt it at any rate so that one grows up physically while one's mind remains undeveloped. How could a man whose mind during the formative years was not allowed to develop, write anything down that would be worth reading? This question haunted me every time I picked up a pen. Fortunately the learning years in New Zealand, Australia and in England re-educated me, giving me a newly formed mind as well as a new pair of eyes. I cherished this phase of my life so much that I made Prem Surin, the protagonist of **Monsoon Country**, go through in lurid details what I underwent in these democratic countries so as to demonstrate the mental reformation and the process of overcoming a crippled mind.

"Now living among the Esarn people on the land on which I was born in my home village, Napo, one could not exist without having sympathy for the silent sufferers. You may say that they don't know any better! On the whole most Esarn people are not likely to complain or to voice their grievances. It's their *karma*, remember? For centuries they have been silent, without an effective voice. Only when they are pushed to the extreme, suffering beyond endurance, do they enter the capital to look for help from the authorities; their gatherings in Bangkok are so far peaceful. Each time they return to their villages with some promises from the government that their troubles would be looked into. But, alas, the promises turn out to be empty, and ironically those governments do not last long either, so

6

then the suffering poor from rural areas keep returning to Bangkok the following summers again and again. Now their plea for help in front of the Government House has become an annual event under the band name of the Plea from the Assembly of the Poor.

I fear that one day, after so many failures to obtain effective assistance from the authorities, they might not bring only troubles with them to Bangkok. Then what shall we do? For now we pin our hope on the fact that the suffering mass in rural Thailand would soon be tired of coming to Bangkok year after year. They should succumb to the notion that nothing could be done to alleviate their plight, that they would hang on to their belief in *karma,* the inevitable retribution, so that they must continue to suffer silently in their communities. The people in power may consider themselves fortunate that the annual assembling of the desperate poor at their doors are orderly and non-violent as opposed to those taking place in some other countries, Argentina recently, for instance. But here, we are indeed fortunate when it has been proven time and again that the rote learning and educational system that is mind maiming work exceedingly well on the impoverished mass.

"Though I do not stand idly by while the suffering poor make their annual plea for help in Bangkok, the voice of my guardian angel comes to my ears: "Don't lead them. Let them wake up and emerge due to their own desperation. Your role is an observer, then write about them as you see them." I heed the voice not only because I believe in my protector but also I want to be alive, at least to finish writing **The Force of Karma.** I keep in mind that more than thirty lives of teachers, the champions of the poor, labourers and environmentalists have been brutally 'liquidated'. As a responsible writer, I am much concerned not only with urgent social issues but also with the plight of those who have been excruciatingly affected by the Moonmouth Dam (Pak Moon Dam) in Ubol. It is difficult to blot out the image of squatting old women and defenceless men and a pregnant woman being clobbered like animals by armed men so that the relocation of the villagers, who were in the way of the construction, could be made. Now the Moonmouth Dam has been proven to be a disastrous flop since it could not generate sufficient electricity as purported at the expense of human suffering and ecological disaster while the World Bank continues to make a handsome return from the loan. I too have made a 'return', definitely not in a financial sense, but in a story: *An Old Man and A Boy.*

"Similarly, *The Gunman* does not stray from the fact that a group of villagers walked peacefully to Wapipratoom District Office in Mahasarakam Province to air their grievances. Their rice fields and river had been made salty by the brackish water from large-scale salt farms owned by powerful politicians and influential investors. When their farmland became salty they could not grow rice, and in Naamsiaw River, fish died. Many farmers had to sell their once arable fields at very low prices and move away to find new land elsewhere. In front of the Wapipratoom District Office, the suffering farmers were battered and arrested and thrown in jail. Yes, for their sake, I protested against such injustice in my own way.

"The majority of the poor people of Esarn remain meek and subservient and through their acceptance of their fate, they tend to avoid making outcries or demands. We know this. Employers know this only too well. Thus it gives sweatshop slave drivers and factory owners an advantage over the silent and meek ones. For this, Thailand's Board of Investment can boast that the country has one of Asia's cheapest production overheads with lenient environmental measures in order to attract investment from abroad.

"Taking it upon myself to speak out on behalf of *the battered silent and meek ones,* choices of tone and styles of speech are opened for me. In my books, particularly **Monsoon Country,** and its sequel, **The Force of Karma,** the current social conditions, the norms, the attitudes and the base on which the hierarchy rests are described along with the social ills, the corruption and injustice. By describing them in vivid detail, I hope to bring to mind what should be corrected or changed for the better. When I wrote: "There are too many thieves in high places, cunningly and shamelessly making use of their positions and power, without conscience but with great capacity for avarice. These corrupt men aim at accumulating wealth as quickly as possible for themselves and for their families, without caring for the good of the nation" I hoped that at least one or two of these broad home-truths would make some Thai readers think. When I talk of the lack of conscience, I aim to make them ask themselves whether it is justifiable to say that conscience is what most Thais don't have. Without conscience, one can bribe or take bribes, can be corrupted and do wrongful acts, without a sense of guilt. The corrupt may still claim that they have not done wrong. Then again it is up to me to make my writings 'acceptable even to lying men'. If it is not acceptable, then it would defeat the purpose.

It cannot bring about change. It cannot change the way *they* think and behave. In that case I would fail as the champion of the downtrodden, the cheated, the exploited and the silent people.

"Why do I write the way I do? Let me explain. In Esarn I was raised in poverty. I suffered hunger, pain and abuse. I had a fair share of happiness as well as sorrow. As a poor boy from Esarn, I was much despised and ill treated in Bangkok. In time I learned that a lot of Esarn people receive similar treatment in Thailand's large cities because many of us are illiterate, penurious and ready to accept any hard work at the lowest pay, without complaint, just like buffaloes. These experiences caused much pain in me. I wince when I think of them.

One may compare oneself with an oyster that suffers from a coarse grain of sand or a sharp foreign matter that strays inside it when it opens its shell. In order to lessen the pain, the oyster secretes a substance to coat the source of pain. After a long while the substance grows and eventually becomes a pearl. Pearl farmers use this knowledge to produce cultured pearls by keeping the oysters on the seabed until they grow to a suitable size, then bringing the farmed oysters up and prying open their shells to insert pain causing matters inside them. You can imagine the pain the poor creatures have to endure for years before they can produce the pearls. The end results are my books, my pearls. When I write, there is a sense of relief. In living in Esarn, I draw my strength. What has been happening here and in Thailand as a whole challenges me to counter-act with writing. The injustice, the unscrupulous suppression of wages and prices of farm produce, farmers losing their land and livelihood through forced relocation to give way to dam construc-tions and to eucalyptus plantations, the deforestation, illegal logging and the pollution of the air and rivers, the poverty and misery of the impoverished people have been taunting me daily. Then came the economic collapse in July 1997. A large number of 'laid-off' workers, who did not receive even the last month of their salaries, not to mention the severance payment, returned to their home villages in Esarn, only to become dependent on those who have previously depended on them. Being unemployed, they hang around their villages, with a hope that they would be called back one day to resume work when the financial situation of the factory owners improves, but to no avail. The promise has proven to be empty in most cases.

To pick up a knife or a gun is definitely not my way for I hope very much that the pen is more powerful than any weapons available for use today."

D.M. Allen and Derek Housman

Thailand in the 21st Century

What happened in France on the 14th of July 1789 and shortly after would not happen in Thailand unless the belief in *karma* is removed. A vast number of Thais believe that in this life if you are poor, crippled, suffering from injustice, calamities or some atrocious attacks, it is a result of *karma* (deeds) done in previous lives. Therefore, their faith in *karma* seems to cushion them against the rough edges and vicissitudes of this life. The acceptance of their fate becomes a norm.

Being stuck in the gridlock of the highly congested streets of Bangkok, one often sees crowds of people waiting, sometimes for an hour or more, to fight for space on an overcrowded bus. One wonders what they feel when they see other people in Rolls-Royces, Mercedes, Jaguars, and BMWs, and what, in turn, do the luxury riders think of the masses waiting for the public transport and the hawkers and beggars clamouring on the pavements.

Pira Sudham, one of the seven children of *the damned of the earth,* as the author saw his parents among the penurious peasants in his home village in the impoverished Esarn region of Northeast Thailand, has waited for buses too, watching the rich ride by in their sedate sedans. He wondered what good deeds these blessed people must have done in their past lives so as to enjoy such riches and good fortune in this one. He also pondered whether there could possibly be a way to counter the force of *karma* or break the *karmic* cycle so as to escape from poverty and ignorance, or whether he had to succumb to his *karma* and a life of the damned all his days.

"A book by a European writer gave me a hint," said Pira Sudham. "When I read the line: *Poverty, like corruption, is a human condition, which can be addressed,* my life was to be forever changed." Starting anew, the author eliminated the *cushions* and the self-deprecating dictums drummed into him in childhood so as to enforce obedience, obsequiousness and mindlessness. He began to make a revolution in his life.

"If *cushions* are taken away from suffering peasants, slum dwellers who hardly make ends meet, and indigent inhabitants, particularly those whose wages or the price of agricultural produce have been severely suppressed and who have been forced to leave their land to give way to the construction of dams and eucalyptus plantations, what kind of revolution would Thailand have?" Pira Sudham ponders.

Bangkok has become the centre of affluence, employment, education and opportunity in Thailand. It attracts landless peasants, prostitutes, job seekers and desperate migrants from all over the country. Over two million of them live in the vast areas of Bangkok's slums. Recently, the drive to obtain wider areas of land to expand eucalyptus plantations and dam constructions has brought about the forced relocation of more than five million villagers in Esarn. As a result it has increased the number of migrants who eventually converge on the capital, thus multiplying Bangkok's problems.

A city of twelve million, Bangkok is choked not only with people, cars, trucks and taxis, but also with poisonous fumes, and disease causing dust and time-energy-money wasting congestion. Not only the chronic health problems but also tensions have increased remarkably in recent years, when farmers dared to gather in order to make their grievances known. Several groups of suffering folk from rural areas marched into the city to ask the government for help. Each time they return with promises, only to resort to another peaceful march the following season when the promises turn out to be empty. This growing activism seems to suggest that Thai society is fast changing. Social tensions grow daily due to the rush towards industrialization, the increase in numbers of migrants in the capital and the decrease in agricultural production. An increasing number of farmers stop cultivating their lands to pursue employment in factories, or are bullied to leave their lands, which can then be used as plantations for the benefit of the pulp and paper industry.

"How long can we keep the poor, the voiceless and the exploited to remain silently submissive, to believe firmly in their *karma*, or make only peaceful gatherings once or twice a year in front of Government House? What shall we do when one day they will no longer walk into Bangkok empty-handed?" the author wonders.

More and more wealthy Bangkok residents deploy expensive, high-tech security systems and hire armed men to guard their hotels, mansions, offices, shopping centres, condominiums and apartment buildings against thieves and intruders.

"Shall we continue to turn a blind eye and deaf ear to the suffering millions? Shall we continue to take the land from them,

12

cheat them, suppress their wages and the price of their produce and exploit their bodies for cheap labour or sexual pleasure? When the poor become desperate to the extreme, losing their land and livelihood, they will end up in Bangkok where the tensions will become increasingly unbearable," the author laments.

Thus, out of the forced relocation of millions of people, the suppression of wages and price of agricultural produce, the forceful drive to gain more land to plant the damaging eucalyptus trees, the corruption, prostitution, child trade, slave labour, the horror of the Thailand-Burma Death Railway during the World War II, the economic crisis in July 1997, the war to win the people in impoverished Esarn in the seventies and the daily grind in the Mother of Gridlock - Bangkok come tales of hope and tales of woe, tales of acceptance and tales of the struggle for survival in the no-win situations that become *Tales of Thailand.*

Peter Manningford-Bohune

Gustav Erne

The Old Man and the Boy

Governed by greed

Swinging their satchels on their way home, five boys in their school uniform chatted excitedly. They had good reason to be jubilant for the day was the beginning of a summer holiday. The road, once a narrow lane, had recently been widened to accommodate the traffic when these fertile orchards would be completely transformed by property developers. At present, signs of the development were still scattered. Remnants of fruit trees and old homes could still be seen where shop-houses and towering buildings left gaps on the roadsides.

Most landowners had sold their properties and moved to give way to progress. In recent years there had been a surge in the construction of high-rise towers, office buildings, condominiums, shopping centres, commercial complexes and shop-houses all over. On Chantira Road only a few old residents remained, winning temporary reprieve from land speculators and property developers.

In front of a dilapidated house, the boys stopped.

"A very old man lives alone in there," the oldest of the youth gang told his friends. Then he kicked the tall wooden gate with all his strength.

"I've never seen him," one boy said as he followed the leader's manly exertion until the wood cracked and broke off and the barbed wire on top fell. But the lock held out.

"I've never seen him either," another boy voiced vivaciously.

"When I was little my mother used to scare me, saying: *A very old man lives alone there. Don't go near the place. He's weird. He likes eating little boys' livers, kidneys, and offal*," the boy who was born in the neighbourhood told his friends who had recently moved in.

"Let's see if we can get him out of the house to show himself," said the leader, sure of his manly fearlessness and group strength.

"To eat the offal?"

They laughed and began kicking the gate with all their might. They rattled it too, shouting *Grandpa! Grandpa!* with boyish sweetness, feigning the innocence of childhood.

Could the ancient warrior be fooled?

The little rascals laughed louder but the age-old wooden house was as silent as ever. Hence, the vacation-spirited lads resorted to throwing sticks and stones to lure the victim. It would be fun to see the mystery solved.

Eventually they succeeded. Out came the head of long white hair. The heavily wrinkled face looked wild with rage. Fire seemed to be consuming the skin and bones while the hissing and cursing sounded ridiculous. The curser could hardly realize that in these days few persons believed in *barb boon koon tose*, (sin, merits, goodness and punishment). But he kept on cursing his assailants, damning them and their parents for not bringing up their young to respect their elders. But the damnation did not produce any effect either. Moreover, the excited brats began to pelt their wobbly target. The staggering creature shrieked and hobbled about. It was indeed a grotesque sight.

The assailants squawked and sniggered before going on their way. So then, with a thought that he had won another battle, the weary victor moved slowly to the back part of the house, heaving heavily as he warily stepped forward. Farther into the garden where lettuce and spring onions and coriander were thriving, the doddery recluse mumbled a sad reproach against the young ruffians and the world, which was encroaching upon him in all directions. Realizing that he had forgotten his walking stick, the First World War veteran vacillated but decided to do without and so dragged his feet towards the clumps of lemon grass and put the curses on the expansion of the city that threatened him with more neighbours and busier streets. He could do without the noise of vehicles and the fumes that were killing his trees. The condemnation was also directed at the widening of the road that ate into his land. He was still very much upset and nervous from the combat with the little demons. His heart wildly palpitated. His hands trembled so. His wizened face set, and his lips tightened. Moving on to the ginger plants, he told them of having been forced to sell his land by a land-grabber who came in a big Mercedes. "Now", he mumbled, "we've to put up with a sky high building on the left and an unfinished construction on the right."

The flowering plants stood rigidly to attention while the palpitating old heart heaved deeply once more to overcome a spell of dizziness. He had to keep still for a while to be well again.

Suddenly there was a noise coming from one of the guava trees. The moribund man sensed an intrusion. Without a walking stick, he could not move fast. This time his legs failed him, and he stumbled and fell. He had to lay down there for some time to regain his breath. When he could rise to his feet, he was afraid that the intruder must have escaped. The hoary-head wobbled; the trembling bony legs did not co-ordinate. Thus he staggered painfully forward; it took some time for him to reach the tree, shading his weak watery eyes against the sunlight that shined through leaves.

"Come down!" shouted the old soldier, trembling from his effort to roar.

The thief turned out to be a small boy whose mouth was full of the stolen fruit.

"Come down immediately, you little imp."

In case the urchin might have armed himself with a sling or a knife, the unsteady veteran looked for a stick. "How dare you," he roared as he beat the air with the dead branch of a guava tree. "How dare you behave as if these fruit trees have no owner!"

When the little imp came down and stood in front of the ex-soldier, it was plain to see that he was not a member of the schoolboy gang. Far from it, this little thing looked more like a starving elf. The skinny boy's stained shirt and shorts were tattered, losing their original colour from wear and tear. Not only the clothes needed a good wash, the boy himself wanted care. Thus, the confrontation was not to be as violent as anticipated. The meek little boy stood submissively, looking down at his bare feet in silent repentance. Nevertheless some punishment must be rendered.

"These trees have their owner," the quivering lips stated firmly, emphasizing the last word. The skin and bones vibrated, not so much from anger but rather from the sense of drama and authority and rights the elder was imposing on the ragged child who remained silently crestfallen.

"You must learn to respect ownership. These trees have an owner!" The aged preached.

"I'm hungry," simply said the boy, whose tears seemed about to drop. Having recently reached the age of ten, he was not guileless. Life for him had been rough and tumbling, being one among a brood of children of an Esarn peasant turned labourer, a casualty among the thousands that had been deprived of their land and livelihood to give way to the construction of the Moonmouth Dam. Since then he and his brood of children had migrated to Bangkok, moving from job to job whenever he could find employment.

For the boy who had to fight for every mouthful, it would take more than a stick from this frail, toothless bag of bones to make him cry. The boy obeyed, opening the palm of the right hand to receive the blows. When the punishment had been rendered, he rubbed his palm against his buttock in a silent demonstration of purported pain. The unkempt little one might have succeeded if the veteran had not turned away, mumbling: "I'm not mean. You've only to ask me for what you want."

Then the forthright veteran wobbled in an effort to turn back to ask: "What's your name?"

"Luke-ped," said the tiny thing whose name meant 'Little Duckling'.

"Ah, yes. You look like a duckling too, a bony one. You must have been starving. Little Duckling eh? What surname, if I may ask?"

"Poonsith."

"From where, boy?"

"From that place," the hungry duckling pointed to the unfinished construction site that was towering over the dilapidated orchard.

"From where originally? I mean where you were born."

"Ubol."

"Ah, so you are from Esarn. All right, you may go."

A pause.

"No, not through a hole in the fence like a thief. Come here! Let me hold on to you, and walk slowly. I shall open the gates for you."

Having let little Luke-ped out, he made a pot of tea, and looked pleased with himself that he held yet a power to command and hang on to the victory over an intruder.

A few days later the Little Duckling came back, knowing that the fruit in the neglected orchard was for the asking. He had to hang around the gates a long time before the recluse appeared.

"Great Grand! Great Grand! I'm hungry!"

A dark movement was seen through some windows of the old-fashioned wooden house. The boy shouted louder than before, putting his face to the crack of the wood so that the old man who was hiding behind a dusty curtain could see him. Cautiously the hermit revealed himself, making sure that it was not another trick to make him come out only to be stoned.

"You said I could have some fruits if I asked you first," Luke-ped reminded him, and watched with mild interest how the bag of bones carefully picked his way with a support from a sturdy walking stick. What the Little Duckling from Ubol did not know was that his newly found Great Grandpa was well over a century old! A few years ago, a journalist wrote about him in a magazine, claiming that he was one of the three oldest Thais alive. And there was a photo of him too, to illustrate the report.

"You said I could..." Luke-ped tried again but the remnant of WW I quickly interrupted.

"So I did." And then he lapsed into stern reticence in order to prevent the little waif from being impudent. It was wise to put a strict measure at the early stage upon their relationship in case it might develop.

The morning sun had made the heavily wrinkled skin almost transparent. It was the wrinkles and the prominent collarbone that put the boy at ease. Who would be scared of this frail and hoary skeleton? So when Luke-ped had filled a large plastic bag with more guavas than one could eat, he climbed down the tree with a bashful smile. He guessed that the guava owner knew what he was up to.

"Aah, you're cunning."

"My brothers and sisters are hungry too," the Duckling apologized for his greed.

"I don't like a horde of children around me," stated the toothless thing, sipping his tea. "I forbid you to bring them."

Thus, a rule was set for future visits, as he had done with many others in the past. But soon strong cups of tea mellowed him. Most times he seemed unaware of the company. The patio where they sat in wooden chairs was designed for space and for being a part of the house and garden. The verdant leaves fluttered, rippling in their reflection of the slanting sun while the mellowness gently carried the lugubrious veteran off, sailing across the tea water towards the Sea of Weariness. Soon his chin sunk upon his chest; the aged drifted softly into the mellowness of his afternoon repose.

In March when mangoes were in season, the Duckling came nearly every day to pick ripening mangoes. These divine fruits were mainly for the owner to give to the woman who came to cook and clean and to the man who called once a week to tend the garden and vegetable plots. The rest of the afternoon would be a time for a cup of tea on the shady patio.

Tea water flowed with time as the Chin Pow Tower cast its shadow over the orchard and the ancient house. Dreams dreamt more than half a century ago were brought back to be dreamt again, to be made more mellow, while the bony hands shook noticeably in lifting the teacup.

Be careful now, old man. It might spill on your white goatee.

"What are you going to tell me today, Great Grand?" the Duckling watched intently as beads of tea dropped from Great Grand's lips.

"Aren't you going to tell any stories today?" the boy persisted for it was nice to be included in the dream.

When the century-old warrior talked and dreamt, he took you with him sailing towards the past, guided by the hand of memories through the mist of age and time.

"Have you studied our history?" Great Grandfather asked, trembled as his throat contracted, making him hoarse. You'd hear a sound like that if someone was trying to open a huge teak door of an old chapel.

"I haven't been to school," Luke-ped replied breathlessly, anticipating the rumble of cannons and machine guns and clashes of arms and the sounds of trumpets.

Then the mist of age and time had come over the watery eyes. But suddenly a sign of life surged: "Aah, I'll tell you about our Great King Rama V who saved the country from being colonized. This period in our history is valuable to me. I learned something from it, used it to save my land from the land scam and speculation. The British, having colonized India, Malaya and Burma, demanded several Thai provinces in the south by the Malay border. The French did the same when they had Vietnam, Cambodia and Lao under their control. We lost great slices of Lao and much land in Cambodia. Would you believe that at one time Luangprabang, the capital of Lao belonged to us? And so were Battambang and Srisopon in Cambodia. Our great king saw that if we did not comply, the two Great Powers might wage war, and we, like Burma, would have lost the whole kingdom. As a result we parted with only those regions demanded by them, and managed to survive that phase in history with the majority of the country intact. Do you see that, boy?"

"Is that so, Great Grand? Is that so?" eagerly said the Duckling, urging the wise old man to go farther on the road of the past.

"It is so. And you'd see I exploited that part of our history to save the larger plot of land when the threats came to a certain point for me to pack up and go. Like a cake, I cut slices on the left and so many more on the right to satisfied their greed."

"Whose greed, Great Grand?" For his father had said that greed once ruled could never be gratified. Father should have known for now he had been made homeless, losing the family land to the World Bank-sponsored Moonmouth Dam. He had lost his wife too. The Duckling's mother was among a group of old men and women who refused to give way to the construction of Moonmouth Dam. When the armed men confronted them and battered them, Mrs Poonsith, who was pregnant, was whipped with a rusty barbed wire, and she died of tetanus several days later. Despite the loss of the family's farmland and livelihood and his wife, the widower, Luke-ped's father, remained a true Buddhist. Having wordlessly accepted that the losses and the calamity were the doing of his own *karma*, he calmly faced the vicissitudes of life, humbly yielded to the cruel fate, packed up and took his children to Bangkok in search of employment.

"Whose greed, Great Grand?" the curious little one asked again.

Grandpa did not seem to heed the repeated question while he was concentrating on pouring tea. His hands were rather firm from the sense of victory and the glory of the past.

"What if they should want all your land then?" the Little Duckling persisted, arching his neck to make himself loud and clear.

"Then I'll fight to the death! And then I'll hound him, his wife, and his children even from my grave! They'll never have peace or a moment of happiness!"

But, years later, it was the creditors and the fraud squad that hounded the developer, who had to hide, after the financial crisis occurred in July 1997.

The teacup rattled against the saucer. This bag of bones had been brave, had fought in the Great War and was awarded a medal. Now the tea water that flowed upon the Sea of Age lulled the dreamy veteran, carrying him away with blood and death and the ruins of history and the greed of men. He yawned and tears of lethargy came to his eyes.

Seeing the familiar sign, the boy wondered where Great Grand could be in his past. Was he saying farewell to his parents and the young wife before sailing off to war? He was part of the token Thai force, marching along Champs Elysées to celebrate the victory. Was he now weeping over the ashes of his parents on his return? Was he crying over the dead wife who died giving birth to a dead child?

Time and again the old soldier repeated these stories.

Watch out Great Grand for the land grabber with his body-guards coming in the grand car…sometimes in a Rolls, sometimes in a Benz. He wanted all your land. You set your dogs on him and his menacing men when they tried to force their way in. But a day later all of your dogs were dead from poison. Tell me one more time about the march along Chongsaylisay in Paree, about Soam and Verdung. Nice sounding names these *farang* cities. Let me hold in my hand once more that rusty medal. It feels good, the glory. And talk of the day you stood your ground with a pistol in your hand ready to shoot at the Greedy Man and his beefy bodyguards, should they have broken in to force you to sell all your land. Would you really shoot them Great Grand?

"Great Grand! Great Grand!" anxiously shouted the little boy, seeing that the gates were unlocked. He sensed that something was wrong when after a while there was no response from the house. How about the patio and the vegetable patch? No, there was not a soul there. He must be in the house then. "Great Grand, are you in there?"

The smell of vice became stronger as the boy went inside and found on the floor much blood, the head smashed, the eyes dilated and protruding. The dead stared frightfully at the child who quickly backed away against a wall. He became dumb with shock and fear. The room was in disorder; papers and decorative items were scattered about and the drawers had been emptied of their contents. In backing out Luke-ped saw the glorious medal on the floor. Pausing, he considered whether he should pick it up and take it away or not. But then he remembered his Great Grand's words: *You must have respect for ownership, for things belong to others.* He rushed out and ran to the workers' shanties without stopping.

The death did not succeed in making headlines in any newspapers, for it seemed just another case of robbery and a large number of people were murdered each day in Thailand. Nevertheless, it was mentioned briefly in a less popular daily:

A World War I veteran has been found dead in his home. It has been alleged that the murder was an attempt at robbery. The police are investigating the case.

True enough, a team of able policemen made a thorough search of the construction sites and labourers' squalid quarters. Finally three suspects were taken into custody. One of them was the Duckling's father.

Luke-ped was thankful for a lesson learned from Great Grand. Had the police found the medal on his person or in the shanty, his father would never have been released. But even then his father and other men had undergone horrible torture that might induce them to confess. The battered men could not work for several days after having been freed. Then the boy's days gradually became just one day tumbling upon another, losing their significance and meaning.

The murder had not been solved but now a number of men came and cut down the graceful fruit trees. A bulldozer was at work leveling the ground. Watching the men and the machine, the Duckling heard in the poignant silence of his heart his Great Grand's lament: "I'm weary, so weary. My old brittle bones would break should I bend much lower than this."

How the old bones snapped! *Did you have to fight them to the death, Great Grand? My father did not fight. He gave in and silently faced the consequence. And we quietly suffered along with him and with our Mum who, like you, lost her life for fighting to keep our land. The blood flowed for a price so dear: To keep the title deed, the ownership to the last. But soon, Great Grand, there will not be any trace of your trees and no sign of the crumbling wooden house. In their place an office tower block is being built for the new generation to walk in and out and to work and to prosper. Would the glorious medal be found one day? If so, would it be known that you won it on the merits of bravery?*

A group of schoolboys went by, laughing and swinging their satchels. They did not stop to wonder what had happened to you and the house and the orchard. Soon, they would forget all about you, about having thrown sticks and stones at you, that you ever lived here.

Then came a Mercedes-Benz from which the victor and two hefty bodyguards rolled out. Looking at the slaves and the machines, the Big Boss deplored: "What a pity that we can build it only now after the cost of construction materials and the price of diesel have vastly increased. And there's a rumour that the Bank of Thailand may not be able to prop up the battered baht any longer after having spent on the defense 30 billion US dollars of the reserves. The baht may tumble very shortly."

True. When the crash came, the construction sites fell into deep silence. There was not even a sound of a crane, whirling and lifting steel rods and slaps, not even the purring of a Rolls-Royce or a Mercedes-Benz that often arrived and parked in the forecourt. Now some three hundred workers sat silently on their haunches on the dirt waiting in the hope that they would be paid their last month salaries.

Luke-ped Poonsith came out of the labourers' makeshift living quarters and loitered among the subdued workers. While there, he heard a foreman tell the leaderless slaves that the fraud squad had raided the developer's office and found that some staff members were shredding the documents. Because there was only one shredding machine, they shoved a lot of papers and account books and files into the lift shaft! And then the Big Boss disappeared. Hence, there was no cash to pay them.

"Go away now," the foreman shouted. "There is no hope of getting paid. Go on! There's no more work here. Go away! Quick! Get out of here! The place will be boarded up and no one can enter. You must not come back and try to break in. It will be illegal! We'll get the police to arrest anyone found inside the building and on the ground!"

But the unpaid labourers did not move. As if being totally mindless, they continued to squat woodenly like dead stumps. Obviously their static state was not a sit-in protest for they had the look of dumb despair, not defiance. All stared vacantly. Such a mute acceptance and voiceless wonder were proof that the age-old process of enforcing submissiveness and obedience at the grass roots as well as the educational system that served as a mind maiming apparatus worked. If not, there was always a trump card to rely upon, and that was the deeply rooted belief in *karma,* in destiny and *'mia culpa, mia maxima culpa'.* After all most of the fledgling labour leaders and trade unions had already been done away with. The question now was how could they be woken up from mute amazement so that they would lift their backsides and go away peacefully?

Eventually the site manager emerged from his portable steel cabin to replace the ineffective foreman. Facing the silent workers, the Chief of the Construction, who held a degree in engineering from a Bangkok university, assumed an academic tone to talk down on the dim-witted labourers. Masterly he explained that theirs was not the only one but among 245 other huge construction sites that had been halted. A fortnight ago over fifty finance and securities institutions including four banks had crashed. The Thai government borrowed 18 billion US dollars from the International Monetary Fund (IMF) so that doctors and nurses in the state hospitals, professors and lecturers in state universities and teachers in state schools, civil servants and government officials could be paid their salaries and to prop up a state owned bank that had over 80 per cent bad loans. Bankers of the other surviving banks had to bite the bullet when their coffers had already been emptied. The vaults were empty due to over-extending loans most of which had become 'non-performing'. It had been revealed that some presidents and vice presidents had approved large loans without collateral or regretfully with faked collateral. Moreover several financiers and advisers had embezzled huge amounts of money from the banks and financial companies before going underground or abroad. On the other hand, the coffers had also been siphoned by powerful suckers, including bankers themselves, to channel the sucked substance to nourish their private projects such as property development schemes, trade centres, business and shopping complexes, hotels, apartment buildings and condominium construc-tions, housing projects, golf courses, and restaurants. Due to the emptied coffers, the banks were not in a position to approve any more loans to the non-bank related entrepreneurs, who were thus left high and dry, as a result. And so the crashed banks had to be rescued. Now you know why there isn't any cash to pay you," the manager concluded. "I haven't been paid either. Neither the suppliers nor the subcontractors have been paid. All of us are in the same boat."

Whether the bare facts managed to arouse sympathy and understanding from the subservient slaves, it was not possible to gauge. Nevertheless, the manager succeeded in clearing the site so that the unfinished construction could be closed down.

Luke-ped rushed out ahead of the despairing labourers, not that he wanted to be at the forefront of the dole queue, for there had never been any dole queues similar to those in some European countries for Thailand had never been a social welfare state. But he wanted to prove the manager wrong. Out he came onto the road and off he ran to the construction site that was once the old man's ancient house and orchard. There, he saw several workers putting up prefabricated hardboard to enclose and protect the unfinished building from trespassers.

"You can't do that! It's not your place. It belongs to Great Grand! You must have respect for other people's things!" The Duckling shouted at the top of his voice at the fence-raising men, who worked on unheeding of the screaming child.

The builders, who often saw the skinny little thing loiter there, believed now that the unwashed street boy was *maitembaht* (not a full penny) and should have been sent to a mad house. Hence, one of them shooed at the little lunatic. Another threw a piece of wood at him, hitting one of the bony legs. While the same man bent to pick another piece of wood to throw, the lame Duckling hobbled as fast as one good leg could carry him back to the labourer's camp. There, he saw most of the laid-off workers and their family members gather to share their sorrow and despair. Where could they go after the developer's loyal minions came and dismantled the living quarters?

"Without the last month's pay, we have no money to buy rice," voiced one of the grief-stricken unemployed.

Some illiterate labourers had been trying to work out quietly in their heads the amount of money owed to them for twenty-nine days on a daily wage of 130 baht (3 US dollars) but it seemed that mathematics was not their strong point. They waited still until the company's men and armed guards came to disperse the jobless 'buffaloes' so that the squalid shacks could be razed to the ground. The silent beings had little time to collect their clothes and cooking utensils into plastic bags and second-hand carton boxes before being dispersed.

Carrying a large rucksack, the Ubol man, Kai Poonsith, trudged ahead of his five children. In a single file they moved along warily, avoiding the on-coming traffic. Every so often the father halted to scan the sky so as to catch a glimpse of a soaring pagoda or a temple spire. When he saw a glittering roof of a chapel in a distance, he hastened his footsteps and told his straggling children to make a beeline for it.

When the Poonsiths entered the precinct of Wat Pai, the Abbot and a committee of monks, who had just finishing their lunch, were coming down the stairs from the stilted *sala*. Underneath this holy hall several homeless families and vagrants had been sheltered.

Seeing the priests, Kai went straight to them and asked to speak to the Abbot.

At a glance, Luangpor Kong knew that the forlorn man and his horde of beady-eyed children had come to ask for a roof over their heads. Recognizing Esarn features in all of the victims of the economic crisis, the abbot, an Esarn born, allowed compassion to get the better of him. He spoke sympathetically: "You, the wayfarers, follow me to my *gutti*, and after I have my tea, you can tell me your tale of woe. I could see in your sad eyes that there is a lot to tell."

Thus the heavy hearted father and his starving, ragged children meekly moved along behind the yellow-robed monks to their living quarters, the *gutti*, some distance away from the *sala*. Once there the monks went into their own rooms, leaving the principal priest with the homeless. "Have you had lunch?" he calmly asked them.

"Not yet, Luangpor," Kai answered, intending not to divulge that they had not had breakfast either.

"In that case, I'd better take you back to the *sala*, otherwise the left-overs will have been eaten by the temple boys and those hungry mouths living underneath it."

Thus, the monk and the scruffy family turned back. Luangpor Kong led the way up the stairs to the lower part of the hall where ten temple boys were taking their mid-day meal. "Boys!" the Abbot authoritatively raised his voice. "Give some food to this family, will you? They can eat here with you lot, before those downstairs would be allowed to come up here."

An acolyte immediately reacted. As a result a spare tray that contained some food was handed to the strangers.

"And as soon as you finish eating, San, you can go to my *gutti* and make me a pot of tea. When I say a pot of tea, I mean bring a cup and a saucer as well. I'll have tea here in the *sala*," Abbot Kong commanded, knowing that time and again he had to teach the temple boys and adults alike to gain common sense, to use their brains, their eyes and their ears. As for their mouths, he did not have to make much effort, except to ensure that they spoke well and compassionately of all beings and things.

Sitting apart from the eaters, the Principal Priest could see how hungry the Esarn children were by the way they attacked the food. *O dear, they have not been taught to use forks and spoons,* the old monk noticed and inwardly visualized his own reckless childhood there in a forgotten little hamlet of Nongplalai (Eel Swamp) in Kalasin Province. But then, due to his anxiety that the temple boys might not leave any food for the vagabonds underneath, Luangpor Kong had to remind them: "Boys, leave some for the lot downstairs. Don't eat every morsel. Think of others, who are at this very moment starving just below you."

He dreaded the day when he might have to turn away the job seekers and the sacked workers and their families, in need of food and shelter in his temple. Lately there had been streams of wanderers coming in successive waves to take refuge for a while and then leave when they could find employment or better places to settle down. Now when the deluge of the economic collapse had been drowning the ill-prepared populace, the temple had become an island for survival. The desperate survivors waited for handouts in daytime and to curl up among stray dogs on the bare concrete floor of the sala at night. What could the old abbot do? It would certainly be against the rule of compassion to refuse food and shelter to the refugees. *Look at each of them now, coming up the stairs to scavenge the leftovers of the leftovers. What a sight! Ah, these are the victims of greed and ignorance and desire, the roots of all our suffering in the world. If only all beings would heed the teaching of the Lord!* The mournful monk sighed.

Soon Luangpor Kong seemed to be relaxed a little by the second cup of tea.

"And now come closer to me, the Ubol people. Do tell how you have ended up here," said he.

The Poonsiths moved further inside the sala to where the abbot was sitting. And then, Kai began his tale.

"I'm not an Ubol man as such, Luangpor. From Amnajaroen, I went every summer with a group of men from my village to fish at Moon River just below the Ubol Township. On one of the fishing expeditions I met a girl of Khongjiam there. After we were married, I lived with her family as it is a way with us, Esarn people. She gave me eight children but three died in infancy. Then she died too. How she was killed set us wandering from place to place and from job to job. It began when some influential men came to our village to coerce us to sell our land to them. They claimed that in a few years time a huge dam would be built at the mouth of Moon River. Our land would be under the water when the dam was built, and we would get very little for the compensation or none at all for being mere village dwellers without any bargaining power. They said we would get more money if we sold our paddies to them. But what they offered us was so little that my wife refused to sell her inheritance to these speculators, who, as it turned out later, resold the land they bought cheaply to the colluding officials at an inflated price. We hung on to our land until we were at loggerheads with the dam construction people. We must yield, they said or else we would be forced brutally to move. In defiance, we gathered, squatting on the earth. Old people too clung to one another for support. My wife was seven months pregnant at the time but she sat among the old people when the armed men came. We, including old men and women, were battered with rifle butts and clubs and rusty barbed wire. They would not spare even the pregnant and the very young. It was the barbed wire that killed my wife and the child inside her. She was cut badly and she died of tetanus soon after the attack. We were made to feel that we were in the wrong, to be in the way of the World Bank sponsored Moonmouth Dam construction. Because there are so many mouths to feed. I must find work or we starve. There was absolutely no job available in Ubol where landless villagers affected by the other dams in our areas and in some other Esarn provinces converged on the town, competing for employment or spaces on the pavement to sell things or to beg. Eventually my children and I drifted to Bangkok, leaving my neighbours to carry on the protest in their hope to have fair compensation and a better deal. Our people did not defy the authorities for human rights since we had not heard of it until I came to Bangkok, but they wanted to be treated fairly, like human beings."

"Was it easy to find work?" the world-weary abbot attempted to steer the battered former rice farmer away from the social-economic-political issues that were too unholy for a monk to contemplate.

"Yes, it was at the beginning, Luangpor. But later on it was scarce. I am prepared to do anything. There is nothing that is too hard or heavy for me as long as there's work."

Early the next day, Kai took Luke-ped with him on a job hunting expedition after having assigned his remaining children to stay put under the *sala* to guard their bags of possessions. Of all his boys and girls, the Duckling was more adventurous. On foot the father led the way along the streets of inner Bangkok, scanning the skies for signs of construction activities.

"Dad!" the streetwise son cried. "If you keep looking up and not down, you'll fall into a gutter or an open sewer or stumble over the broken pavement or the motorcycles will run over you!"

"I didn't know that motorcycles can use the footpath to dodge the traffic," said simple Kai.

"Oh yes, they can. They paid the police so much for those sleeveless jackets, which they wear to indicate that they are for hire. The people who sit on the pillions are their paying passengers. And having paid for the jackets, the taxi motorcyclists are protected. Don't you know that Dad? And why do you keep looking up at the clouds? Jobs are not advertised in the skies, you know?"

"I'm not looking up at the skies. I'm looking for cranes on top of unfinished construction sites. If the cranes are moving, then it means the building work is still on, not stopped. I'm not as stupid as you think I am. And don't try to be so clever. You don't even go to school. From now on shut up."

Nevertheless the hopeful Esarn man sought all the building sites whether the cranes above moved or not. Unfortunately those he found were securely boarded-up. Most of the unfinished construction sites looked derelict, exposing the protruding steel to rust. There was not a soul in all of these decaying projects.

At certain congested areas, the father and the son saw some long queues of people spilled out into the streets to withdraw money out of their banks rumoured to be the next to crash. But for not having any savings, Kai Poonsith sensed a relief.

With some relief and high hope, Kai walked on. His hopeful heart pounded with the tempo of the traffic, while his scruffy son babbled by his side to cheer him on. Soon the two victims of the Moonmouth Dam lost their ways in the gridlock of Kroongtep, the Celestial City of Angels.

Two Thai Women

A drama in four acts

1

The first woman to appear on the scene is Salee Boonpan, known to the neighbourhood as a *mianoi,* a minor wife or a kept woman. Some of her neighbours preferred to refer to her as a *rented* wife. *Rent* had been applied to women of Salee's profession since many American military men stationed in Thailand during the Vietnam War had rented Thai women as temporary wives.

When her keeper was not paying her a visit, Salee passed the time alone in her small wooden house at the end of the lane. The house was rented.

The fact that she lived in a rented house put her in a certain status. It indicated that she had not managed to own a house out of the arrangement. Furthermore, the fact that her man came to see her in a taxi meant he was neither wealthy nor influential, and certainly not a high-ranking official who inspired dread. Besides, the observation that he visited her very seldom pointed out that the woman was not his favourite. Moreover, she might be losing his favour and would soon be discarded.

These facts were useful to the shopkeepers in the lane, whose calculating minds had to account for some profit whenever possible while safeguarding any loss through *non-performance* credits. At the same time the neighours would keep their keen eyes open for what the woman might make a 'back of the house' sale. The landlord too would make sure that she paid her rent. It was only fair that these good people took such measures. To them, if the girls next door work in bars, it would be wise to find out what kind of bars, whether they were in dock areas or in certain streets frequented by foreign residents and tourists, whether they were 'high class' or not.

In the case of Salee, the good neighbours had not seen any new furniture brought in, nor heard stereo sounds, nor seen her wear any jewellery. There seemed very little that the *mianoi* would sell in a hurry. The only thing she had ever sold were a television, a transistor radio and a bottle of imported whisky. These days the woman hardly left her house. Many believed that her keeper had already deserted her.

"But that rented woman is still beautiful," deplored a shop-keeper to his wife in private while counting the cash after the shop had closed late in the evening.

The second woman was Nipa Pitayapunsith. Her letter preceded her arrival. It read:

My dearest Salee,
I miss you so very much. It has been a long time since we parted. I am now living and working in Pattaya. I am worried about you, wanting to see with my own eyes how you're doing. Is he still good to you?
Looking forward to seeing you, my dearest.
With much love,
Ni

Lying on the wooden floor of her house, Salee smiled at the thought of Nipa, of the past. The smile, though sardonic, brightened her face. At the same time, she tossed ideas backward and forward regarding the roles she would play when meeting Nipa.

The afternoon, like most time, had been boring. There was hardly anything to connect her with the outside world. The house swelled in the heat. The room became an oven. Her empty hours unfolded. There was nothing much to do except to eat, sleep, wake up and wait.

Salee went to the dressing table. It seemed reassuring to contemplate her own features in the mirror, combing her long black hair. She was still very pretty, yet it was her beauty that had been the cause of her downfall. It began when a well-dressed, seemingly rich woman visited her village. The city woman came to look for a few young girls to work for her as maids in her Bangkok home. Susceptible to promises and the lure of city life and earning income, Salee's mother allowed her daughter to go with the woman.

While Salee contemplate her past, she longed for something piquant or sour. To make herself presentable to the outside world, she powdered her face and applied lipstick. To go out of this silent, sweltering house to buy a pickled mango, pineapple and guava, gave her a sense of purpose. She would also buy a copy of the most popular newspaper to read all about gruesome murders, horrible accidents, movie stars and parties in social columns in which she might recognize some of her former clients. Should there be another *coup d'etat,* shop radios would be emitting revolutionary songs, decrees, warnings, and exciting patriotic vows.

Anticipating what the world outside might have in store for her, Salee eagerly donned her plastic flip-flops. But then the arrival of Nipa deprived her of any possible excitement.

The plump, aging procurer had not changed much, a little more rotund and uglier perhaps. To put across to her former collaborator the sheer joy of their reunion, Nipa effortlessly flustered, exclaiming: "Salee! Dearest! I'm so glad to find you looking so well," she shammed. There were tears as well.

"Why, Ni, what do you expect of me? Shouldn't I look well?" Salee asked, glad that she had put on some make-up before Nipa's arrival.

Meanwhile Nipa's eyes darted to estimate in a flash her colleague's material wealth. She wasted only a few seconds.

"Haven't you got a ring?" Nipa sounded amazed, scowling in disbelief.

The younger and more winsome woman did not quite understand.

"A ring! Ring on your finger!" Nipa scolded abrasively. She rounded her lips and sucked her teeth with displeasure.

"I don't like wearing rings," Salee attempted to explain.

Nipa put aside her handbag, hissed and then bared her teeth. "It does not matter whether you like wearing them or not. You should have got one out of him. What a stupid girl you are. You allow this gritty grotty man to keep you this long and you don't even get a ring out of him! Get anything! A ring, for instance, and it should be diamond too."

"Why diamond?"

"You're silly. You're even more stupid than I thought," Nipa snapped.

It seemed useless to educate this thick peasant girl. Nipa moved about the room, inspecting the furniture. Her hand glided from one object to another while her brain calculated values. Salee followed Nipa's movement; in her eyes, she saw not only Nipa but also a horde of brothel owners, pimps, murderers, thieves, drug traffickers, and uniformed men who had lived off her flesh. She also remembered hands and feet raised to strike her at any sign of unwillingness. How she used to scheme for a way to escape, to return to her village. But after a year they removed her from the front line, replacing her with teenage girls, freshly procured from the country.

Thereafter Salee had been permitted to walk the streets with Nipa. Later Nipa, who had always been enterprising, branched out on her own and paid for Salee's freedom.

"Let me take care of you, Salee, for you're still young and beautiful. Think of me as your aunt. We have only to look after each other now." Nipa sounded genuinely concerned.

But for the price of freedom, Nipa aimed to own the bought woman for life. Salee had not been completely worn out; a period of grace would bring her back to life. With Nipa's persistency, shamelessness, guile, low cunning and experience, she could build up her own brothel. Salee would be her very first girl.

Now Salee recalled another point of her life. The two of them had spent hours in one of the beauty parlours in preparation for New Year's Eve. As they stalked their prey, Nipa caught sight of an urbane, middle-aged man and went at him: "We are looking for a good restaurant," she cooed. "Would you be so kind as to recommend one to us?"

The fish was nibbling at the eye-catching bait. He himself had intended to dine locally, and since they were similarly inclined, wouldn't the charming ladies be his guests? Once seated in the eating house of his choice, the women felt certain the evening would be successful.

"My niece is from Esarn," Nipa minced her words, each of which was expertly coated with honey. Also, she bent slightly towards the man to arouse intimacy and confidence.

Salee took the hint and thus acted a role of a naïve Lao girl who was shy and meek. When she spoke, her Lao tongue sounded authentic.

However, the client had proven to be a tough customer. It took the dexterous woman almost two weeks to clinch the deal. Since he wanted to have a *mianoi*, Nipa had to change her mind about setting up her own house. If he wanted a *mianoi*, he should have one, but Nipa waned to make a good profit out of it.

Nipa had helped her friend set up a house in a quiet lane on the city outskirts. Having also made extra money from telling lies to her customer about the costs of furniture, kitchen items and the monthly rent, Nipa decided to embark on a new venture. She left the Heavenly City of Angels for the beach resort of Pattaya, a modern Sodom where she had been living during the past years.

"This is not much of a home now, is it?" Nipa was saying; her voice broke into Salee's bucolic mind.

"I'm quite happy as it is."

"I bet he doesn't come often now. He might have another girl somewhere," Nipa sneered.

"He's been very busy lately and on top of it his wife is ill," Salee lowered her voice to suit a sad state of the affair.

Indignantly placing her hands on her hips, Nipa uttered: "Do you believe him?" Her throat contracted and her harsh voice broke.

"Of course, I do. I'm one of his wives too. Why should he lie to me?"

Nipa had to scream: "What! You talk of love and loyalty? I'd rather see a diamond ring, a car, an air-conditioner, a refrigerator, an electric fan and a television set. Now where is your television? Where is the radio? Have you sold them?"

Salee played mute. Nipa sneered knowingly: "These are all the things I bought for you before I left. Perhaps your love and loyalty have got the better of you and you've told him the real rent so that he'd give you less monthly allowances. My dearest, you're still too young to get stuck with this mean bastard in an empty house."

"But why did you set me up with him?" the naïve little woman had to inquire.

"Don't blame me, my girl!" Nipa flared up.

She had to change her tune when she remembered why she had come. Reaching out for the younger woman, she cooed: "Listen. I've a plan. If I didn't love you like my own niece, I'd never have helped you. Next time this miser of yours comes, tell him you had a letter from home, that your mother is very ill and you have to go home to look after her."

"But my mother cannot read and write and I cannot go home now," Salee stated some shameful facts.

"I'll write the letter myself in case he wants to see it. A miser does have a petty misery mind. Then you can come to me," Nipa smiled the famous Thai smile. Then she prattled on: "Now tell me, are you going to ask him for anything?"

For the life of her, Salee did not know what to say.

"A big amount of money for the poor ailing mother, for the fare and..." Nipa prompted.

"Of course," agreed Salee.

"And a ring," Nipa added breathlessly.

"Why the ring?" Salee seemed innocent enough.

Nipa screamed: "I told you before, it's a capital gain! Get it out of him. Use the opportunity! Tell him you need it to prove to your folk that you're respectably and legally married. When you go home for the first time, you need a proof to gain face, not losing face. What a dum-dum you are. The wedding ring will be the proof. Stupid!"

Salee had to admire Nipa for being far-sighted. The two women grinned at each other. Then Nipa decidedly disclosed her *Pearl Harbour Attack* Plan. "My poor girl," Nipa sighed, stroking Salee's shoulder. "If I could be with you all the time and take care of you, no man could take advantage of you," she ended the disclosure of a catalytic scheme.

2

The plan worked out wonderfully. Salee arrived at Nipa's one room apartment in a high-rise hovel in Pattaya.

"How much money did he give you? Did you get *it*?" Nipa could not wait to ask.

"Get what?"

"The ring! Dum-dum."

Impatiently Nipa waited as Salee unpacked and produced a small plastic box.

"Diamonds!" Nipa's greedy eyes gleamed. Her heavy breasts heaved and the pores on her squat nose glistened. But the ring the protégé had secretly bought to pacify the craving guardian was indeed silver and zircon.

"It's just glass!" Nipa's predatory eyes suddenly faded at the discovery.

"How would I know? He told me it was valuable. It used to belong to his mother," innocent little Salee defended the offending ring.

"The mean bastard!" Nipa spat, believing that she and the women of Thailand had been cheated by the like of such a brute. But towards the evening, her vengeful mood changed. "You're still very beautiful," Nipa repeated her well-learned line as well as speaking truthfully for once. "In fact, I'm quite envious of you. Often, I wish I were as pretty as you," which was another truth.

The sight of sex-crazed tourists instigated Nipa to persist unabatedly in her relentless efforts to snatch her share from the lucrative beach resort. She was growing old, and had made little money out of the Vietnam War from which tens of thousands of people had gained their great fortune. That war was well over and the mighty air bases in Udorn, Ubol, Nakorn Panon, Korat, Takli and Utapao at Sattahip were no more. But now there was Pattaya where the mighty mark-carrying Germans, the strong pound British, the godfatherly Russians had colonized the resort. Every so often one heard people brag of striking gold, that dealing with the Europeans was far more enriching than with the Americans. Besides, the Americans only rented their women while the Germans and the British tended to take their Thai women home with them.

As for Nipa, she would not retire just because she was a little too old now for the trade. "I'll snatch what I can for my own," she determined, sharing the same determination as many of those who held ministerial posts. Her hope rose as she looked at her young and winsome accomplice.

That night the two hopeful women strolled along the crowded streets of South Pattaya. Salee was amazed to see so many *farangs* walking in the streets, drinking beer in open-air bars, beer gardens and restaurants. At a beer bar, Nipa darted inside and attached herself to a big *farang*. "You see Hot?" She meant Horst. The burly beer-bellied European shook his head, avoiding eye contact with an unsightly whore, who had passed far beyond the use-by-date. As if she did not exist, he resumed gulping down another mouthful of beer.

"He no come?" Nipa persisted.

The blue-eyed giant shook his head more vigorously.

Defiance, not disappointment, became Nipa's tool. It appeared quite darkly in her vicious, hungry eyes. "Swine!" she swore venomously. Returning to her young colleague, she vented: "Just to think that I spoke to *it* so nicely."

It was quite normal for many Thais to reduce white men to *it*.

Being two against thousands of women of the same inclination, Salee and Nipa became lost in the throes of human confluence as they moved from bar to bar in search of Horst. Throughout Pattaya the ready women were keen for business. Gays and tomboys worked blatantly among drug peddlers, pickpocket experts, stealthy procurers for paedophiles, hoarse-voiced transvestites, jabbering hawkers, German beer-bar owners, Russian godfathers, British pimps and hooligans. Among these the duo felt quite at ease. But the evening proved to be unfruitful. They could not find Horst.

Nipa and Salee slept in the next day. At noon they went out for piquant papaya salad and monosodium glutamate spiked noodles. In the evening they dressed, painted their faces and applied cheap perfume to their persons and thus they were ready to face the tough competitions. That night they were in luck to find Horst in one of the open-air bars. Immediately Nipa clung to him as if she had known him for a week. Because Horst was big and tall, the procuress had to stretch herself up to the host's hairy, expansive chest to cajole: "You like? She number one!" Nipa made a thumb-up sign and winked.

Salee acted her part, parting her lips slightly to look prim, demure and alluring. But her hastily put on dramatic role seemed to have gone to waste since Horst was busily buying them beer.

"No freelancers here," the bar manager said grumpily.

"These are my friends," Horst argued strongly.

"They're freelancers. I have over a hundred women working here. You can have any of them, but no freelancers walking in here!"

The German sex tourist and the Thai pimp scowled at each other for a brief moment to test the strength and power of the opponent. It was Horst who relented. He took his women out of the beer bar and off the trio went into the confluence of crowds and the throes of traffic.

A day later Nipa said to Salee: "You'd be better off here than in Bangkok. Here, I can take care of you, and between you and me, we'll be more than just surviving. We'll make money. Lots of money."

Salee seemed unenthusiastic.

"Look, Dum-dum. The whole place is booming. Everyone is rushing in!" Nipa coaxed.

"As you know, Auntie Ni, I still have my husband," Salee sadly laid down a well-known fact.

But dexterous Nipa had another D-Day plan. "You go back to that miser of yours. Don't worry my pet, it'll work," Nipa concluded, patting her *niece* on the back.

The following morning Salee went back to Bangkok. Nipa's scheme somewhat amused her, making her optimistic. Days passed while she waited for her keeper to visit. When he came, she endured his sexual demands. Twenty minutes later on, when he had time to look around, he wondered: "What are these *farang* bank notes doing here?"

The sight of a lean, middle-aged Thai fingering dollar notes brought the image of Horst's hairy, hefty bulk to her anxious mind, while combing her long silky hair at the dressing table. Without meeting his eyes, she followed Nipa's line: "I fancy them."

A minute went by, then: "Whose blond hair is this?" which was exactly what Auntie Ni believed he would say.

"What hair?" she inquired blandly, but tightened her lips in anticipation, sensing that the tempo of the drama was quickening.

"Look!"

Salee pretended she could not see any hair in his fingers and suppressed a contemptuous laugh at the sight of the despicable nakedness that could not be compared to her hunky Horst's. The dollar fancier allowed all the time the little man wanted. How he childishly worked himself up into a rage! "For beauty sake put your clothes on," Salee suggested smilingly. She had to ad lib: "You look disgusting!" But she would not dare to ad lib further that hefty Horst was her heart's desire now that she had truly *known* him.

"You have been playing tricks with *farangs*, haven't you? How do you like those big apes? Big enough for you?"

Seeing in her mind's eye her beefy Horst standing nakedly by her side vaunting his manly prowess, Salee could belittle the raging skeleton with a vulgar remark, which made the little monkey hit the roof. He struck her in the face, sending her to the floor. She uttered a loud cry, and the pain was real.

Putting on his clothes, he spat out his disgust, saying she had disgraced Thai women by going to the gorillas. "Don't expected to see me again!" were his final words, which Nipa had also anticipated.

The wooden house shook at the banging of the door. Battered but relieved, Salee rose to her feet. Her face had a glint of a cynical, beguiling smile. No more play-acting was required. Thus the sordid episode of her Bangkok life came to an end.

Pattaya became her home. Once more the two women lived together. One possessed a keen instinct for survival, low cunning and a calculating ability while the other had desirable features and an enticing body. The latter had also learned how to fabricate her tales to arouse sympathy to milk more money from her clients. To some customers she had two children to keep in school, an ailing mother for whom she fended. Her folk often became ill, and there was an undying ambition to open a beauty parlour of her own. To Horst, Salee wanted to run a restaurant in which he should invest. Her dramatic life and longing took on more vibrant colours and lurid details with Nipa's dexterity and the progress Salee herself made in English. Each tale seemed real and fitted her like custom-made clothes. All she had to do was to adopt certain expressions to appear on her woeful face to suit the stories selected.

Meanwhile the mysteries surrounding foreigners became less intriguing, and their physiognomy, which inspired anxiety at the beginning, had now been made familiar though very close contact. She was fascinated by the *farangs'* rite of sunbathing. So she became involved in it, rubbing sun-lotion on her temporary hosts, sensing also how such a simple act could increase intimacy. As time went by, she could walk into first-class hotels in Pattaya, north, middle and south, to flaunt her shapely, bikini-clad body by the swimming pool of the hotel in which her man stayed.

It was all very well for the hotel staff members to pretend that they did not see her as long as the hotel guest paid an extra 500 baht a night to keep her in the hotel room. She should be proud to be a part of the attractions of which Pattaya could boast. Yes, she and thousands of women like her, were marvelously responsible for bringing in tens of thousands of tourists a year. And she was now enjoying a fair share of them. For instance, Klaus kept her for several days and once took her with him to the coral islands on which he and she made a lurid performance for a friend of Klaus to make video recording and photography for which she was paid handsomely. Not only the amount of cash received, but Salee remembered well also the pleasurable boat ride, the lunch that the hotel provided in boxes, that Klaus' face and body turned lobster red after only half a day in the sun, and she had rubbed so much sun-lotion into it.

Emil walked the length of Jomtian Beach with her. At one point he wanted to pull her into the water and make love to her in the sea. "For once, I want to do it in the Gulf of Siam," said he. But she would not go into the water. "I'm not stupid," she told him. "Only tourists, who don't know how polluted Pattaya Sea is, swim in it. All the untreated sewage from hotels and shop-houses goes into the sea, my dear. I won't even dip my feet in it." But then she yielded, hoping that the tip would be an extra large one. As a result he and she suffered badly from skin rash, and had to see a doctor at a hospital. While there, they had to have their blood checked as well.

Derek stood out in her memories. Dilek, which she uttered as if it was a Thai name (correctly pronounced 'Direk') would not demand a favour from her, not even once. *He's a 'pudee ungit'* (an English gentleman), she recalled. All he wanted was to talk with her, asking her all sorts of questions, taking her photograph (which later appeared in a widely circulated British daily). "We talk, talk, talk. No do what men usually do. Talk cheap. Yes?" She had taunted him and wanted him to abuse her so as to earn her keep. There was only little money in talking. At best a meal in a side street eatery might be thrown in. Her Dilek was an unrequited desire, not so much for his body, mind you, but for his pale delicately clear skin and rosy cheeks, the doing of the peculiarity of the English climate. *If only I had Dilek's complexion!*

Salee remembered well another longing of hers.

Nils was more or less like Horst but more gentle, and not so much hair on the body, but what a body! The sheer size of his made her moan and groan, but Nils believed that she simulated to urge him on. Nevertheless, with him she had enjoyed good food and wines in which she had begun to take delight at posh hotels and in pricey restaurants in and outside Pattaya.

Jonas was a queer fish, but she yielded all the same to his outlandish ways. For such weird performances, she made a killing according to her simple, rustic calculation.

And then Horst returned the following year. Salee was happy to be his woman for three weeks! During that time, no other girl could attract him, taking him away from her, no matter how cunning and good at languages they were.

No, Salee did not mind the contemptuous looks of the hotel guests and others. Fortunately she neither suffered from AIDS nor any contagious disease. She believed that she was quite clean for a woman of her class. But it was a sense of permanence that she dreaded. After twenty-one days with the same man who said he wanted to marry her and take her to Germany, she feared that certainty was threatening her. She could not laugh off the prospect.

Before leaving for Germany, Horst gave her a considerable sum of money. Nipa demanded a fifty per cent cut and suggested that her niece should go over to the hotel and demand commission from the extra 500 baht a night Horst had paid for three weeks to have Salee up in the room.

"But that's the commission the hotel made from us. It's like pimping, you know. You can't take commission from pimps," young Salee tried to educate her avaricious, aging aunt. She also intended to stop walking the streets while waiting for Horst to come back and marry her.

Nipa had to laugh: "Just because you spent some weeks in a luxurious hotel, now you want to behave like a madam for the rest of your life!"

It bothered Salee to ascertain that Horst would actually take her to his country called 'Yeramun', so far away from Nong Bua Village where she was born. It was transience with which she could cope. In her professional life, men came and went, and she moved on, working for the next meal, the next man, attaching no importance or value or sentiment to encounters. But then why did this big cuddly bear called Herr Horst want to marry her? Could it be love or just a fashion in Germany to have an oriental wife?

L-O-V-E, Salee saw the word being spelt out in her troubled mind.

But she felt something towards Horst. This *something* worried her. It could hardly be the money he gave her, could it? Was it then the way he gentlemanly treated her, behave decently towards her, *love* her even? She could dare the contemptuous glare from those who considered themselves more decent than she, when he was at her side.

"This is a first class family hotel. You can't allow this type among our children," some wives complained to the hotel manager for they did not know that the hotel had already pocketed the extra 500 baht a night.

When Nipa's fifty per cent share ran out, she pestered Salee for more, and pressed her to return to the streets of Pattaya rather than waiting for Horst who might not return.

"He will," Salee sounded confident.

"Damn it!" Aunt Ni shouted. "Don't talk to me about love and loyalty. We're a free people. Thai means free. Free! Free! Free! You hear? Why should you be faithful and loyal to a *farang*. *It* is never one of us!"

Whenever Nipa wanted more money for gambling she staked household items. Salee tried to end this practice. As a result the two women argued heatedly. Their argument fumed into a fight eventually. It was only then that Nipa discovered Salee's strength and determination. Retreating to the far end of the corridor of the mean block of the high-rise hovel, Nipa screamed to air her pain: "I picked her up from the gutter, looked after her and cared for her like she was my own niece. How ungrateful can she be! Hear me well! She is an animal. She is vile and low and stupid at that. She is stupid enough to believe that a German wants to marry her just because he fed her for a few weeks. I tell you, *it* won't come back to marry her. We'll see who'll be starving."

Salee continued to wait for Horst. Her loyalty and faithfulness to him was measured by the length of time his money lasted. After it was all spent, she considered that she was free again. Yes, Thai means free.

4

A year after Salee had returned to her home in Nong Bua, Nipa unexpectedly appeared. Nipa's arrival caused quite a stir. It happened one June afternoon when an old run-down vehicle halted in front of some shabby shops where several ragged urchins and mangy dogs were scavenging. A dusty gust of wind followed the little bus and stirred some men from drowsiness. They shifted and wiped weariness from their eyes. Nipa turned to one of these lethargic men. "This is Baan Nong Bua, isn't it?" she wanted the confirmation.

Her audience remained silent at the sight of this opulent-looking woman in trousers. Her city clothes, Central Plain Thai accent, rouge, painted nails, jewels, pouting red lips and paunch made her look weird, garish and menacing. An old man nearest to the madam stirred. He understood her but did not wish to try to speak for shame of his Lao tongue. Thus, he merely nodded, coughed and spat.

"Do you know Salee, Salee Boonpan, then? She used to work for me," Madame said grandly.

Surmising that the lady must be influential, representing perhaps the power of the Masters, the gathering lapsed into the submissiveness that peasants normally adopted when confronted by officialdom or well-dressed city people.

"Children, take the lady to Sa's hut," another old man ordered the curious youngsters.

One daring, half-naked child took hold of Nipa's totebag and began to lead. Among the throng of jabbering boys, our Pattaya grand dame followed with the air and grace of the high born as dogs yelped and chickens squawked out of their way.

When Salee returned from watering her herd of buffaloes, she betrayed no obvious pleasure at seeing Nipa, already quite at home amongst her admirers, young and old, from various neighbouring huts.

Salee's mother sat humbly on the wooden floor under the presence of one so extraordinary, glittering and gracious, exuding wealth and civilization as opposed to the subsistent, poorly clad dwellers of a forgotten Village of the Lotus Swamp.

"Hello, Sa! Here, I am!" Nipa uttered joyously.

Salee did not return the greeting. She pulled hard at the buffaloes, forcing them into the pen under the hut. The beasts, startled by this unusual congregation, refused to budge. So Salee hit one closest to her with a bamboo twig. Only then did she express any anger and this produced results. Finally she penned the animals and wiped the perspiration from her forehead.

Salee had not expected Nipa to turn up in the village, nor had she ever considered how she would cope with such a situation.

Having observed Salee's features and her healthy natural colouring, Nipa could see that the cycle had turned the former protégé back to peasantry, that Salee had recovered. She could pass for twenty, just a little robust and rustic for the present.

"Dearest Sa, you must have been working hard in the sun and the wind!" Nipa exclaimed. Turning to her attentive audience, she bewailed. "I could never understand why Sa left me. The work was nothing, and we lived well. Many young girls would have envied her if they had known."

Several wizened women simultaneously remarked on Salee's lost city life. What a tragedy to fall back to the drudgery of village life.

"I hope she'll return with me to be happy again in Kroongtep, the Heavenly City of Angels," cooed Nipa while Salee came up to the hut and sat nearby. Patting her long lost niece on the shoulder, the procuress continued: "You good people may not know that I've adopted Sa."

Salee's trembling mother struggled within herself to voice words of gratitude for such great kindness for it was so rare that a peasant girl would have the chance. The crone shook with an effort to express an appreciation that would be acceptable to the lady from the Divine City.

Meanwhile, Nipa rambled on: "Did Sa ever tell you all about how we lived in Bangkok? Never? Not a word about our big house in Sukhumvit, the most posh area of Bangkok or about our villa by the sea?"

Everyone seemed to be murmuring. Salee shifted painfully inside her loose cotton blouse. She forced a smile, made an excuse and went into the cooking part of the hut. There she sat on the floor and blew onto the embers, trying to revive the fire in the earthen stove. A flame flickered whilst the smoke and soot brought tears to her eyes.

After dinner, weariness from the day's work lulled her. The darkness was soothing and consoling, yet Salee still fretted. She tried not to disturb Nipa who was sharing the same corner. She was troubled as she contemplated the pattern of moonbeams coming through the broken bamboo partition. Only yesterday, with the natural turn of seasons, life at peace had seemed eternal. But now her sordid past had arisen before her eyes, carrying her away on a sea of memories — names, faces, words and deeds committed in desperation and duress, in daylight and darkness alike. To Salee, it did not matter providing her mother and the inhabitants of the Lotus Swamp Village knew nothing of her past life in the Heavenly City of Angels and in Pattaya. The end result, the money orders sent, had meant survival for several of her people under this thatched roof.

No, I don't wish to return to the gutter, Salee assured herself. And she said as much to her former colleague the next day. She tried to explain a little: "My mother, as you can see, is now old and ailing. My uncles and aunts are poor and hopeless by themselves. I'd like to be married to a man who could help me with the work in the field." Salee laughed and arched her graceful neck. The idea of trying to catch a husband locally made her girlish.

"Oh well," Nipa sighed. "But having come all this way, I may as well try to take one or two girls back with me. Won't you help me convince some pretty faces that there are good jobs and a home waiting for them in the magical Kroongtep?"

"You can try," Salee did not succeed in attempting to hide her agitation.

Somehow the remark seemed a challenge to the old professional.

Early in the morning, Nipa set off from hut to hut. By mid-day her catch amounted to one willing tiro (an orphan) and one reluctant beauty. The reluctance was simply because the rice planting would soon begin. All the help the family could have would be much needed. But Nipa skillfully brushed aside this obstacle; she had only to paint a glowing image of the Heavenly City, gentle living and money.

The mere mention of magical Kroongtep had a fantastic effect. It had always been the home of affluence, attracting adventurers and landless peasants alike, to seek fortunes and employment - their share of the nation's wealth within its limited radius.

The two pretty girls were soon to leave for the Celestial City. The dwellers of Nong Bua believed it was indeed their good luck, merits accumulated from past lives. Their reward was the chance Nipa offered to take them away from the quagmire of penurious peasant life.

To send the two lucky girls off in style, the village elders organized a *soo-kwan* (soul binding) rite. Several old men and women sat solemnly, mumbling words of blessing. Witnessing the ceremony, Salee became more wretched. The knowledge of the life that awaited the two innocent ones in Pattaya made her wince. Despair drove her out of the village to brood under a banyan tree beside a sluice. Above her, darkening skies rumbled with thunder. Squatting among the tree's gnarled roots, she snapped a fallen dead branch and flicked pieces at a dragonfly hovering over the murky water. "Would I dare?" she murmured.

A crow circled and then arched its wings to land, screeching: Gar! Gar! Gar!" the sound that means in Lao: "Courage! Courage! Courage!" Salee froze, statuesque, as she tried to decide. At the water's edge, small mud crabs rushed to and fro. Frogs watched her tensely from their hiding places. The creatures were quite relieved when she rose and eventually walked away. Courage! Courage! The crow sounded encouragingly, observing her departure.

Back in the hut, Salee told Aunt Ni that another beauty from a nearby village wished to be taken along. Greed flashed across Nipa's face. "I think you should see the girl before you agree to accept her, Salee suggested. You mightn't want her since she is approaching twenty. But she's astonishingly beautiful. Yes, beautiful and petite, she is too. If we leave now, we could be back before it rains."

"Thanks for helping your old chum, darling," Nipa sounded pleased.

Many witnesses saw the two women leave the village. Late that night the inhabitants of the Lotus Swamp were thrown into great excitement by the news that bandits had killed the city woman. Death, particularly a gruesome one, made fertile ground for rumours and superstition. Men and women gathered during the following days to talk of the robbery and murder. Some said that Salee ran wildly into Nong Bua, bleeding from wounds. They said the body of the city woman was found in a thicket, stripped of jewellery. She had been stabbed to death.

Once again the village elders organized a soo-kwan rite for Salee to bring back to Salee's flesh and blood her soul that might have taken flight due to the frightening experience. In the headman's house, sages, women and children, young men and girls all gathered on the floor. Sitting among them, Salee seemed heavy with humility. The doddery soothsayer cleared his throat to signal that the ritual would begin. His voice rose gently. Crouching towards the chanting senior man, Salee trembled as several people bound her wrists with the blessed cotton thread. A feast followed, specially prepared for the rite and to feed the policemen from town sent to investigate the case. They sat apart from the villagers, enjoying their meal and whisky with the headman and his wife attending them.

When the policemen had been fed, Salee was summoned for questioning. She meekly crawled on all fours to crouch humbly near to the most senior officer, bending her head as if she had to talk to the wooden floor.

Taking control of herself, Salee began: "Nipa and I came upon three men in the woods. They were strangers and, to judge from their accents, they must have come from another province. They wore black shorts and black cotton shirts. Two carried a small chest balanced on a bamboo pole. The other had a knife. The one that was holding a knife asked us where we were heading, and I told him. The strangers paid special attention to Nipa and her obvious wealth. You know she wore a lot of jewels. The travellers followed us. I did not see anything suspicious about them. One often comes across strangers passing our part of the country. But when the man with the knife overtook us and blocked our way, it was plain that he intended to rob us."

"Slowly, slowly," said the senior policeman.

Salee paused so that he could catch up with her statement. While she waited, hardly anyone stirred. Then the officer said she could continue.

"The other men tried to prevent us from running away, forcing us to leave the track and then marching us into the depths of the woods."

"Would you recognize these men, if you saw them again?" The policeman burped rather loudly.

"Yes. I had a good look at all of them while they waited for Nipa to take off her jewels. But then she decided to fight though we did not have much money on us and her jewels were fakes. She was a big woman and very strong, so it took all of them to cope with her. While the scuffle was on I ran as fast as I could. One of them followed me but there was the sound of buffalo bells somewhere and I cried for help at the top of my voice. The herd of buffaloes scattered at my cries and sudden appearance, but there were no herdsmen about. My pursuer did not know that that was the last herd let loose in the woods to be rounded up for ploughing in a week's time. He was frightened off. I kept on running."

Then the headman directed another villager to make a statement. Feeling important, the appointed man sat up straight, expanding his chest: "Sir, Salee came running and shouting into the village. Her clothes were torn and she was bleeding. It took us a long time to make any sense out of her. The headman was away, and I confess that we were afraid to go into the woods at night. We waited till the morning to look for the Bangkok woman. We found her stabbed to death."

The headman then gave an account of how they had disposed of the body. His account was brief, for the headman's wife and servants had by now brought another generous helping of Esarn sausages, *yum-nue* (spicy beef salad) and a new supply of whisky. The policemen formed a new circle to eat and drink.

Weeks passed. Some people still felt sorry for the two girls who, having lost their chance, had to content themselves with village life now that Madame Nipa was dead. They would not be able to live it down that they had missed that once in a lifetime opportunity to set foot in the Heavenly City.

Then the monsoon rain came pouring down, flooding the rice fields. Planting rice, knee-deep in the muddy water under the glare of the sun, Salee stretched up to ease her aching back, breathing in deeply the fresh clean air. A soft breeze revived her with the scent of rice seedlings that blended well with the smell of the newly turned soil. Her mind spelt: L-O-V-E, and then its eye saw Horst smiling at her, coming towards her. Then she felt a warm wind enveloping her as his image faded away.

Salee had no way of knowing that Horst had perished in an air crash some 35 minutes after the aircraft had taken off from Bangkok International Airport.

"My love," came out of her lips without her having to make an effort to form and utter them.

The swaying bamboo grove at the fringe of her fields whispered the promise of a good season. Salee attempted a smile, but then she caught her reflection in the water.

If Nipa had not been dead, she would have returned to Nong Bua from time to time to lure unsuspecting girls into a sunless prison where days became chains, and cruelty came from hands, feet and fierce, soulless eyes that threatened: "Try to escape and we'll kill you. They will bring you back to us if you go to them for help. They work for us!"

Salee could hear Nipa's dying scream; it shattered the placidity of her domain. A crow glided and perched on the grove, reminding her with: Courage! Courage!

"Gar! Gar!" she answered back hoarsely.

A handsome young man, who was planting rice not far away, looked over. Aware of his gaze, she smiled at him. Only then his boyish face bloomed into a refreshing, innocent smile.

Father and Son

More than a generation gap

Father has become an embarrassment, particularly to a son who has spent over ten years as a student in England. At heart Father is still a shopkeeper who made his way up from being a noodle hawker, starting off with a push-cart, a charcoal stove, a dozen noodle bowls, twelve pairs of chopsticks, ten spoons, and two buckets of water. Some years later, through sheer hard work and thrift, he could afford to rent a shop.

During the Second World War, he made his first million, selling scrap metal to the occupying Japanese military forces. From one shop, he opened three more in the heart of Chinatown. Then no one dared to call him *jek* (Chink) after he moved up the social scale to a status of *Tao Kae* (senior proprietor). His huge fortune was made during the Vietnam War. He had a lot to do with the ability to monopolize money exchange services set up in American air bases in various parts of Thailand and in the warships anchored in Thai waters, as well as supplying various materials and providing accommodation to the US military personnel on rest and recreation.

Father has a wonderful gift for making connections in high places, particularly in the military hierarchy. He entertains lavishly a number of invincible generals and awe-inspiring government officials, formidable bureaucrats, and mighty members of the cabinet. Bankers dare not take him to court. When one of his factories was burnt down along with 200 workers, mostly females, who were trapped inside due to locked exits, with 400 injured, he did not have to face any law suits. To replace the burnt property, he built and opened a new manufacturing plant under a new name and in a new location, while the injured and the relatives of the dead have been trying vainly for some compensation. He rationalized that workers, labourers and peasants are stupid. It was indeed fortunate that the lot of them believed in *karma*, in the bad deeds done in past lives so in this life they suffer retribution. "Because they truly believe in *karma*, in the acceptance of their fate, it's easier for us to manipulate and control them, making them work long hours, and keeping them in submission and subsistence. I just hope that they won't wake up," he told his family members during dinner. Just then the Anglophile son felt a lump in his throat, and food refused to go down without help from a cup of Chinese tea.

In contrast to his father, an image of noble Lord Woodborough, the father of his fiancée loomed, while in his ears the son heard a well-remembered voice of the peer: "My dear chap, without conscience we might as well go back ten thousand years and be beasts of the jungles!" The paragon of probity and nobility could not believe his ears that, charming as they appeared, the Thais were in need of conscience. "Without conscience, there is neither sense of right nor wrong. One can do all sorts of sinister things, and without a sense of guilt one can go on committing awful deeds and still claim that one is right and innocent. My dear fellow, I trust that at least they uphold certain ethics, honour and some level of righteousness in your country," stated Lord Woodborough.

The rich young Thai did not quite remember how the subject of conscience came into their conversation over their port one evening at Woodborough Hall.

Meanwhile Father, a self-made man who made a rags-to-riches story come true, has been amassing wealth by leaps and bounds. He could well afford to send his sons and daughters abroad for education and at very exclusive schools and colleges too. Yet throughout the years his taste and behaviour have not changed much despite the fact that he has become one of the wealthiest and most powerful men in the land. He still has the mentality of a shopkeeper. As for a sense of good taste, he owns several large diamond rings, diamond-studded Rolex watches, two Rolls-Royces, five Mercedes Benzes, three Jaguar cars, a yacht, a palatial mansion with a big swimming pool in Bangkok, an imposing beach front villa with a fantastic swimming pool in Rayong along with teams of chauffeurs, servants and gardeners.

Because Father does not go for fine things in life, the Anglo-Saxonized son wishes that his papa would read at least one book in his life, enjoy classical music, art, and fine wines in addition to certain expensive cognacs and Scotch whiskies. The son would also like Father to observe European table culture and to adopt European manners when meeting and entertaining European business contacts, customers and bankers at home and abroad. The elegant young man does not know how to take it when Father clears his throat, spits and burps loudly. Father also adheres to his old habit of taking off his shoes and lifting one foot to rest on the knee of the other leg and shaking it while eating. The embarrassed son cringes while Father slurps his soup.

When the daughter of Lord Woodborough came to visit him and her soon-to-be father-in-law some months ago, it was obvious that she was not at all impressed by the family's perplexing wealth, for she insisted in moving out to spend the rest of her stay in a first-class hotel. In her hotel suite, the young lover heard his wife-to-be say on the telephone to her confidante in London: "It's either red or pink, quite garish really. You should see huge wooden furniture all inlaid with mother of pearl, and you should hear the sound of throat-clearing and spitting. No, no, I don't mind people being ordinary, but this is absolutely vulgar and common. Moreover, there is something sinister about the old man. Everywhere he goes, at least two body-guards hover over and around him."

A fortnight later the young millionaire got an e-mail from his lost love from Woodborough Hall saying how sorry she was to break off the engagement, the reason being she could not stand the mosqui-toes, the heat, the poisonous fumes, the dust, cancer-causing fungus spores and the chaotic traffic. For the life of her she could not see how she would be able to live in such a place which is aptly called Kroongtep, the Heavenly City of Angels!

The heartbroken young man could not understand why his beloved was not at all comfortable in his magnificent mansion, was not at all impressed by the opulent wealth. He could have easily bought her diamonds, a new Rolls-Royce, a grand manor house in England and whatever her heart desired. But after a while he considered that his aim at rubbing shoulders with the peerage was, after all, whimsical. Yet he keeps on wondering. He wonders whether it was his father whom his lady had rejected. The son sensed that his love also cringed in the dining room of The Ritz when the two of them had dinner with Father on one of his visits to London. Some diners pretended they did not notice when father did his routine of taking off his shoes, slurping his soup, burping, and loudly clearing his throat. Thank goodness, the old man did not spit that time. Nevertheless, the vulgar tycoon managed to milk 975 million of British tax payers' money out of the Commonwealth Development Corporation as a grant from an 'aid' scheme to fund one of his new commercial ventures.

Of all the places in London, it has to be at The Ritz, the son was bemoaning to himself when Father held his knife and fork as if they were weapons being used in martial combat. Having gone through tortures at one of England's most renowned public schools, the son made an attempt at showing Father how to hold his knife and fork. "At the school I was rapped on the knuckles for holding the knife like a pen," said the son. But father did not seem to take the hint.

Father has his pride. In one of the most expensive hotels in Paris, he would not succumb to the arrogance of the *maitre d'hotel*. He ordered the most expensive wine on the wine list. After a sip, he rejected the bottle.

Many a time the Westernized son has thought with concern of Father's vulgarity and sinister appearance. Of course, he is not refined by any European standards. His face brings to mind an image of a movie gangster in Chinese films, not the look of breeding seen on some of his European counterparts. But then it is not fair to compare Father with some of the noble-looking English peers, for the man aims only to make money in any way possible, not to be refined, elegant and noble. To father and hundreds of tycoons like him, money means power and it calls for respect, regardless of how one acquired the wealth. With a lot of money, he can subjugate others, bribe and win monopolies, contracts, concessions, licenses as well as holding great influence. When one becomes a multi-billionaire, one can do what one likes and can get away even with murder. Crudity, hideous features, sinister air and bad manners can be overlooked.

Looking from another angle, one has to admire Father for what he has achieved in a short time. In his youth, in a narrow dusty corner store he used to work from dawn till midnight, selling, carrying goods and keeping stock. There was hardly any time to eat; to him eating was to tuck the food in, gulping the food down as quickly as possible so as not to waste time. He hardly took a day off, and 'holiday' was a foreign word. He scoffed at people who needed holidays, or even a day to go away for relaxation. To close the store for a day means no money made that day, and to leave the shop to an employee to run was to take the risk of being cheated.

Since the son still wishes to marry an English girl regardless of her standing, whether she is of high birth or from a lower order, rich or poor, his father has to change some of his crude habits and learn to conduct himself in manners acceptable to European high society.

So then he starts to educate Father in some subtle or not so subtle methods known to him. At one point he engaged a wine expert to come and conduct wine tasting and appreciation for Father's benefit. But they have been of no avail. One may argue whether it is fair to impose the European way of fine dining and ethics on Father when it should be easier to make European business contacts and visitors learn how to use chopsticks, slurp soup and suck in noodles from the bowl. One thing about Father is that he has always had his ways of getting back, of taking revenge.

From the penthouse of the sea-front hotel which he has just taken over, Father scans the shore and the poolside where a large number of guests are swimming and sunbathing. "I make my money from fools," he chuckled.

Yes, it is true. Father has been building his fast expanding empire from fools. To him, fools include bribe-hungry ministers, kick-back takers, loan-approving bankers, a myriad of corrupt civil servants, high-ranking government officials, development corporations of certain countries, stock manipulators and buyers, joint-venture partners of failed or non-existent schemes, business partners, affiliates and shareholders, partners in crime (not to mention professional hitmen, gamblers, brothel-goers, prostitutes, drug traffickers, pushers and addicts), unsuspecting consumers, factory workers, labourers, illiterate peasants at large, tenants of the office towers, buyers of housing estates and condominiums, motorists who buy smuggled and diluted petrol, and last but not least, sex tourists who use his hotels.

However, Father has made many enemies, particularly with other awesome *chowpo* (godfathers), who would not stand idly by and watch him rake in money when he enters their territories to compete with them in their special lines of business. But father does not seem to fear them despite several attempts on his life. The one he dreads is his own son who has been trying to turn him into a man who reads books, listens to Bach, Beethoven and Mozart and occasionally takes real holidays. Why must he have a benign and graceful air? What is the use? He should continue to get rid of his strong competitors, labour leaders, prominent activists, protesting school-teachers and unwavering foreign auditors by intimidation, strong-arm tactics, and the ultimate terminators – the hired gunmen.

But definitely the son wants his dear father to become ethical, less greedy, and genuinely patriotic to the country in which he lives and operates so as to help safeguard the country's dwindling forests and prevent petro-chemical plants, pulp and paper factories, sugar mills and cement plants from polluting the air and rivers, and most of all to cease all land scam activities, logging and encroaching on forest reserves. Now that Father has gained so much power as a super rich, he might meet a member of the royal family of Great Britain one day, being a recipient of 975 million under CDC's aid programme. The son suspects that Father has declined the invitation to tour Finland and Sweden as an honoured guest of Finland's export credit and bilateral aid agency and one of the world's biggest concerns in the pulp and paper industry because he is extremely diffident when it comes to meeting and speaking with Europeans. The truth is Father abhors speaking English as much as eating pickled herrings.

To Father, the pedestal his Etonian son has for him is too high (and he is a rather short man too). Against his son's relentless efforts, Father, who has by now invested heavily in China to establish over fifty companies, finally has to put his foot down with: "We Chinese will soon rise to greater power than any peoples on earth. What we say and do will hold. The Europeans and the Americans will have no right whatsoever to impose their values, their beliefs in the quality of life, their concept of human rights and their concern for freedom and environment on us. They shall have to adopt our values, taste, habits and behaviour just as we have been copying theirs all this time."

The son wonders whether Father would live long enough to see the day when China becomes the ultimate power, taking on the world, for he may not survive the next attempt on his life.

Father and Daughter

A study of avarice

To the late-riser, the morning seemed bleak. At nine when Sunita, clad in a white, fluffy bathrobe, came out to the patio of her seafront villa, the sun had already changed the sea's mood. The breeze stirred the fronds of coconut trees that lined the beach while the frangipani stood darkly dappled with white flowers, some of which fell into the swimming pool. Somehow the sight of the gardener cleaning the pool, while his small cassette-player/transistor radio kept nearby was loudly playing Esarn music from his favourite recording, annoyed the woman. She had told the housekeeper to make sure that the idiot must finish his work on the beach side of the estate by eight o'clock of each day, particularly when she was in residence. This measure was aimed not only to ensure privacy but also to prevent the Lao-speaking Esarn peasant turned gardener from gawking at her or her guests as they sunbathed by the poolside. You never knew what a yokel, raised in poverty in such an awful and hideous part of the country, might have thought and what he could have done when temptation was too much for him. Somehow this morning, her fragility had suddenly been shattered by the blasted *mohlam* song blaring away and the lady of the house went to the poolside, picked up the offending wireless, and bashed it several times against a bole of a golden-shower raintree. As if she was not satisfied with the soundless state of the damned thing, she swung it down on the ground and then went after it, stamping vigorously on it as if she was absolutely consumed by the envy of someone else's simple joy. It did seem a rather unladylike exertion, that stamping and kicking which she repeated several times before returning to repair her shattered self on a rattan chair on the calming patio.

When the maid appeared, kneeling on the marble floor at a respectful distance, the riled, fiery mistress could not help vent further her anger: "I've told you several times to make sure that the cretin does not work by the pool area after eight. How many more times do I have to tell you? In what language did you tell him? Was it in Thai or in Lao? Since you are also from Esarn, speak to him in Lao, he may understand it better!"

"He has neither a watch nor a clock, *ka nai,*" said the trembling housekeeper. It was obvious that the cowering woman was familiar with the flaring temper, the foul moods and the abrasive croaking of her Ladyship. Having been reduced from serving in the palatial house in Bangkok to a servant in a seaside villa, the poor soul was being made more humble once again.

"I'll get him a watch, and take it out of his wage. Tell him that. Have we plenty of fresh orange juice?" Sunita said ruefully and in the tone of those who had the prerogative of great wealth.

"*Ka nai.* Plenty for four," tremblingly answered the squatting woman, who was getting on in years.

"I want a glass now."

Sunita stretched her slender arms skywards and yawned. Then she leaned forward to pick up *Women in Love* from the coffee table. Distinctively the Gulf of Siam murmured. The sun had become strong enough to cast shadows of clouds onto the shimmering sea. The sound of the water lapping the shore and *Women in Love* helped sooth her irked mind. These days she could easily lose her temper due to the increasing tensions from the volatile financial situation and the insidiously manipulated stock exchange plus a court case involving a sibling feud. On top of them all, her thought of suing her husband for divorce had been gnawing at her. It seemed too that those whom she had liked were attacking her behind her back. A journalist joined in as well, making a nasty remark in a social page that at a party she had been seen adorned by a diamond necklace that had a thirty karat blue diamond pendant called 'Tear Drop' after its shape. How could a name like that become the thin end of the wedge? That bitch of a social columnist dared to make a snide remark in the gossip column: *We have been blessed with a chance to gawp at Sunita Panichakulkosol-Charlton's diamonds, particularly the one called 'Tear Drop', aptly named since thousands of the slaves in her family's factories have shed tons of tears in a recent strike to demand some improvement in working conditions, welfare and an increase in their wages.*

These days she could not put on a piece of jewellery without being criticized! Oh dear, oh dear. And what had her collection of precious stones to do with her slaves in factories? Envy, pure envy. "I'll sue the bitch," Sunita reconsidered.

There was no point in trying to read while she could not stop thinking of other things. Putting the novel away, she looked around the patio as if to allow something else to catch her attention. She checked the cushioned rattan chairs and a sofa to see if they had been neatly arranged, whether the glossy magazines on the coffee table had been attractively displayed. How nice it was that the colour scheme of cushion covers matched that of the flowing bougainvillaea on the terraces. Awnings and colourful beach umbrellas had been put up. Four chairs surrounding the round table were empty, however. She could not see her husband, Charles and the guests, Edwin and his wife, Rebecca.

Sunita saw on the wrought iron table at the open part of the porch, tea things left untended, and thus guessed that Charles and the visitors had had their breakfast. Where could they be then? Her ladyship got up and walked towards the sea, leaning against a ceramic rail, scanning the length of the beach. No, there was not a single soul in sight. Presuming that all three of them had gone into town to get a copy of the English language newspaper and freshly baked bread from a hotel bakery-shop, she returned and slumped into a couch, sighing deeply. It had been a miserable week, having to go into and out of courtrooms. Now it had become obvious that the fight for the properties and top positions in the empire would be a long drawn out war among her half brothers and sisters. Fortunately her father was quite partial to her, the only surviving child of his favourite *mianoi,* a concubine.

Mrs Charlton had always considered herself to be strong and practical, and to think that she was jealous of her husband's long-standing friendship with Edwin Pennington was totally unacceptable to her. Yet when Charles and Edwin met, whether they were in England, Hong Kong or in Thailand, she felt left out, that she was turned into an outsider, circling at the fringe of their close relation-ship. Sunita Charlton was not ignorant of their public school days at Winchester, and the Oxford years; she knew too that in their halcyon bachelor days they lived together in Knightsbridge, their habit of going to concerts, theatre and operas together. When the firm for which the two friends sent Charles to Bangkok and Edwin to the Hong Kong branch, the distance seemed to increase their desire to see one another as often as possible, like the present for instance. The depth of their relationship had touched her at first, and thus she accepted that Charles needed to keep in touch with his friend, but when their togetherness had alienated her, she felt hugely hurt. To add another injury, the company of Edwin and Rebecca, the epitome of English mentality and attitudes, had always made her feel that she was after all a Thai, a wog, in their midst. She resented this so much that she could turn her Anglophilia into an aversion.

Sunita herself was educated in England, having spent six years there, a period to which she alluded as her 'Anglo-Saxon' years. Consenting to her parents' wish, she returned home and all was well for a while until she finally admitted that she could not watch Thai television and put up with the stupidity and childishness, that there was no theatrical life, no concerts, and most of all she had no friends. "I am utterly out of place in Bangkok," she had written to one of her English girlfriends. Yet, in the same letter, she did not fail to mention a life style in the great house of the Panichakulkosols with a team of servants, chauffeurs and gardeners at her beck and call. Gone were her days of having to cook and wash the dishes, doing the laundry by herself in London.

The Panichakulkosols had become in a span of only thirty years one of the wealthiest and most powerful families in the country. They had established and profitably run an extensive and ever-expanding chain of commercial enterprises, property developing concerns, automobile dealership, the operation of a fleet of ships and fishing vessels, several hotels and resorts, nationwide petrol stations and convenience stores. Not long after Sunita's home-coming, suitors wasted little time in seeking her hand, but they soon realized that she treated them as boys or under-developed men with a little boy's mentality, that she was too outspoken for being a Thai lady. In other words, she had become too much of a *farang*. Some rejected ones claimed that she had lost the cherished quality of Thai women, who should remain 'the hind legs of an elephant. By this they meant that she should stay behind, remaining a submissive and obedient follower instead of being at the fore. Many a wounded one had to bear the brunt of her open contempt: "Me play the traditional role of a Thai housewife? Forget it." And she had laughed in their faces: "You think I'd stay home doing nothing except being a mother to the children of a childish man?"

Hence it was not a surprise when she finally chose her husband. At the time the choice did not cause as much a stir as some might speculate. In modern Thailand such inter-racial marriages were becoming acceptable in high society. Rumours had it that the wedding reception held in the flagship of the Panichakulkosols' hotels was definitely one of the grandest, most exuberant, most glittering Bangkokians had ever seen. One could imagine the amount of gold and diamonds that adorned elegant and charming ladies of high birth and of wealthy and renowned houses that evening. It was surprising, however, to see that most of the rejected suitors turned up among the thousand guests; some of them were heard extolling Sunita's virtues. Of the bridegroom, they paid unreservedly their compliments on his exceedingly good looks, that he was eminently suitable. None would insinuate that he could be a foreign adventurer, seeking fortune through marriage. So they gallantly circulated, trying not only to keep on the good side of the bride but also to renew their favourable contact with her father and some of the cabinet members who were guests of honour.

After Sunita's honeymoon had been well over, those who loved her had hoped that she would be happy and settled, seriously taking part in running the family commercial enterprises. But she disappointed them. For when Bangkok became boring and stifling, she flew back to her home in London. If not London, then she resorted to her Rayong beach villa where she brooded as she was doing now.

Now the opulent mansion and the bougainvillaea and the coconut palms brooded and sighed along with her. It had been a happy marriage for a long while, but somehow after their children, one son and a daughter, had grown up and were in boarding schools in the United Kingdom, she and Charles began to drift apart. Once or twice a week Charles would come home in the small hours or sleep somewhere else. Recently she had engaged a private detective firm to confirm her suspicions and to come up with some evidence which she could use in court. For 50,000 baht, she had a report that her husband regularly drove his personal car to a certain hotel's multi-storied car park, made a telephone call from his mobile phone, and waited for the hotel's general manager, who soon turned up with bags of food and wines. The two men then went to a luxurious serviced apartment for which the suspected paid monthly rent, and spent the evening or the night there. During a monitored period of one month, Charles Charlton arrived with the hotel general manager with bags of food and bottles of wines (champagne was also mentioned) at the apartment and spent the whole night there on the 10th and on the 24th...

Lately Sunita's father talked seriously to her that he wanted to transfer Charles Charlton from a managing directorship status in one of the core business companies to be a general manager of a subsidiary firm dealing in consumer goods. "Not that I don't trust him," the patriarch had said. "But there are things he should not know. He'a *farang*, and never will be one of us."

Not long after such a conversation had occurred, the father broached again the same subject, but this time in a more urgent imperative tone. Yes, she would sue her husband for divorce, but on what grounds? It would not be easy to push aside and put out of her life any man who had been sitting on a heap of gold and diamonds and billions of cash (half of which was in the collapsed *baht*). When the Englishman was no longer an in-law, he would have no claim on anything. The daughter would replace the *farang* in all of his previously held top positions in the family's business corporations and companies. According to the father's promise, Sunita Panichakulkosol (without Charlton attached to her name) would not have to lift a finger to get rid of the first wife's sons and daughters. All would be hers eventually.

While thinking of her father, her mobile telephone rang. "Oh, hello, Papa." Sunita tried to sound cheerful. After a long pause, she voiced anxiously: "No, I haven't read any newspapers this morning. the Morning Post doesn't normally reach here until eleven or twelve." After another pause: "Of course, Papa, sue them. Sue Siam Post, Reuters and Kaosod, for every *baht* they have!" She was obviously trembling while moving to and fro, pressing her tiny phone against an ear. "I'll come as soon as I can," she ended the phone talk.

Rebecca came out from her bedroom, exclaiming teasingly: "What's that all about? Cracking your whip again so early?"

But Sunita did not seem to hear or be aware that a guest had entered the verandah. Picking up *Women in Love,* the English visitor peered at the cover. "This is a rather serious book to read on the beach over the weekend, isn't it?

Without turning to acknowledge the presence of Mrs Pennington, Ms Panichakulkosol (in whose mind the marriage had already been dissolved) brusquely remarked: "Just to refresh my memory of the film" and left it at that.

It was too early for gin and tonic. Champagne would do nicely though most unsuitable for an occasion on which headlines of and articles in the day's newspapers, Thai and English and Chinese alike, could be so damaging to her father, to her too, and to the clan members who bore their surname.

"Oh, yes, the film was fantastic, wasn't it?" mused Rebecca, unaware of the inner tension and shattering nerve in the other. "Hunky Oliver Reed wrestled with dishy Alan Bates. Both stark naked. Yum! Yum!"

Then the English woman walked down to the beach to stand in knee deep in the rolling sea water, lifting her pale blue cotton dress up above the lapping tongue of the sea. Sunita kept the sight of Rebecca while her anger against the British sense of superiority rose. It was they, Rebecca and her husband, who could talk facetiously about the filthy rich in Thailand and in Hong Kong where they lived. And it was Charles, who joined in with: "No, no. Not filthy rich but sinisterly rich!" How dare they, the foreigners in her house, sneer at her in her face, making outrageous remarks such as this while they wallowed in the wealth of her family, eating her food, drinking her wines, using her cars and servants!

Then there was the sound of a car being parked in the garage. Some minutes later, Charles and Edwin appeared in similar tennis outfits. "Hello, darling," the husband greeted his wife, tossing the Morning Post on the coffee table, and then bent down to turn the front page up so the bold headline of *Billionaire Witanawong is refused US visa* could be seen from where the woman was standing. Without a word, Edwin Pennington left the friend to join Rebecca on the beach. But then Charles followed as if he was the other's shadow.

When the trio sauntered back after the lapse of almost an hour, the poor wealthy woman noticed that the two men almost reached the same height of six feet, but Edwin had more delicate features and was slightly less in weight as opposed to Charles' refined looks and broad shoulders. During the salad days of their marriage, Sunita had mentioned to some Thai women who gawked adoringly at her prince charming: "And he's very public school, you know."

"Tea or coffee?" Sunita asked the three as if she had not read the Post.

"Tea, please," said the trio in unison as if they had not talked about the news behind her back.

The lady of the house called for the maid and ordered tea for the English and *kaotom talay* (seafood rice soup) which she had alone in the dining room while Charles and his friends took tea by the sea. After a while Charles came to his wife and said: "Let's take Rebecca and Edwin on a boat and have a picnic on the island." When the wife remained silent, concentrating on her breakfast, the husband pleaded: "It would be so nice for them. I'll ask Boon to make sandwiches and I'll pack *foie gras*, smoked salmon, caviar and a few bottles of champagne in ice boxes, then we'll be off."

"All right," the wife replied nonchalantly, without looking up while she contemplated the bowl of *kaotom*.

Then one of the drivers was dispatched to the fishing village of Baan Shan to secure a boat. The guests were told to take their suntan lotions, towels and flip-flops. Soon a small fishing boat approached the villa, making a spasmodic tut-tut-tut sound as the boatman tried to nose it up the beach for the party to climb on board.

The grinning, youthful helmsman wore only baggy black trousers which Edwin thought were pyjama trousers. The half-naked native was in fact a fisherman, earning extra income by taking tourists to the island whenever he is not out to sea. Barefooted, he was busily steering his boat away from the land.

The wives were spreading their large blue fluffy towels on the deck-chairs before sitting down on them, facing seaward. While the boat was nicely gliding on the slightly choppy sea, Charles Charlton uncorked a bottle of well-chilled champagne as Edwin brought out glasses from a picnic basket. When they were skirting the island, Charles attempted to communicate with the ever-smiling Thai youth, pointing with the hand that was holding his drink: "Too many tourists on the beaches on this side, go farther and we'll find a beach with no people on it, *kaojaimaikrap?*"

The handsome fisherman smiled broadly, nodding.

"Well done, old chap," Edwin mentioned to flatter his friend though he did not know a word of Thai.

"Awful," uttered Sunita. "Charles still needs to go back to his Thai classes. He doesn't even know the difference between *kobkoon* and *kobjai.*

"She's only jealous of my Thai," Charles told Rebecca. "The Thais don't even understand *her* Thai."

Against that remark, Sunita flashed her hateful look, glad that her mind was momentarily taken off the headline and the report of the Post. Eventually their boat arrived at a deserted sandy cove. Here, the sea was mild and the water was sparklingly clear and blue. The sandy beach beckoned to them. Having anchored and stopped the engine, the humble youth took out a cigarette and began smoking. He looked content enough to remain within his own world, while the world of the rich *farangs* seemed millions of mental miles away. But for once, he took a sly look at the bikini-clad figures and entertained his own thoughts. He had taken uninhibited *farang* tourists here several times and some of them had divested themselves of all their clothes to sun themselves!

Charles and Edwin dived almost at the same time into the water, swimming together to the shore, while the women took their time. By the time the wives could wade towards the dry land, their husbands had gone to the other end of the cove. Picking up shells by the lapping water evoked Sunita's childhood memories of her time at Huahin with her father whom she had successfully taken away from the children of his *mialuang* (major wife) to spend time exclusively with her and her mother at their beach house. Father was not a billionaire then, but he was on his way to becoming mighty in the world of trade and politics.

At this point, Sunita turned to look for Charles and saw that he and his friend had transformed themselves into a pair of ancient Greek athletes, wrestling on the sand. It took a wounding moment for her to say: "Just like those in *Women in Love!*" Not caring whether Rebecca had heard her or not, she hastily turned and walked in the opposite direction.

On the way back to the mainland, Ms Panichakulkosol looked so sullen that Mr Charlton had to whisper to Mr Pennington his guess of what was troubling her. So the English played dumb and drank the rest of champagne while the Thai sulked all the way. At home Sunita went straight to the master bedroom, but when Charles followed she swung to face him head on, eyes glaring and her quivering mouth demanding hysterically: "I want a divorce!"

As if he had been expecting such a scene to happen, Charles said calmly: "I'll agree to that if you let our children keep my family name which is still clean and honourable so that they can travel and enter countries which your father cannot. It wasn't the headline in today's paper that opened my eyes. I've been hearing rumours, and as a matter of fact, several foreign correspondents have told me openly about the allegation. When he asked me to go to Los Angeles to bring the body of one of your half brothers who died in a car accident to Bangkok, I did not have to guess why your father could not go himself. Your father.."

"Stop! You leave my father out of this!" Sunita did not attempt to muffle her cry. "Get out! Get out of *my* house!"

After Charles had gone, Sunita snatched her handbag from the dressing table and left the room. Her husband was not aware that his wife had not come back from wherever she went off in a huff by car until dinner.

"Then why didn't Tanom drive her? I saw him just now, in the back of the house," Charles raised his voice, scowling at Boon, the housekeeper.

"*Naipuying* took the car key from him," said the frightened servant.

At the dinner table, the host made an excuse to his guests that his wife had gone back to Bangkok to be with her father who needed all the comfort a man in such a predicament might require. His choice of wines included Dom Perignon 1982 to celebrate his forthcoming divorce.

It was not until the next morning that Charles learned of his wife's fatal accident caused by a head-on collision with a truck some twenty kilometres from her palatial home on the beach of Rayong.

A Prisoner of War

Working on the Death Railway

Born on the 24th of June 1921 of John Henry and Elizabeth Ward in Great Yarmouth, Norfolk, a seaside town on the East Coast of England, I was the oldest of six children. Father was a packer by trade and a band member of the town's Salvation Army. Before her marriage, Mother lived in Canada and South Africa for many years. Though times were hard, they managed to make my childhood a happy one. I attended the Salvation Army and, at a suitable age, joined the band as a drummer until I left school at the age of 14.

At that age, life in our green and pleasant land seemed so assured and the happiness so permanent that there were very few incidents to challenge the notion. We held band practice twice a week and the feeling ran high when we played at the Citadel meetings. On Sundays we marched, playing, to the market place and on the promenade in the summer. Decades later, when life became fragile and extinguishable at any moment by the enemy's sword or by a snake bite or ravaging malaria and cholera in a Thai jungle, I brought back time and again those memories from the hidden depths of my heart as I lay on the ground with my head on a piece of wood used as a pillow. Fond memories of the first time such as when I wore the Salvation Army uniform, the sound of the band, and the band's first engagement, a concert in Reedham, a village ten miles from Great Yarmouth. Against the hum of cicadas and the howls of wild animals at night, the tune of The Old Rugged Cross, sung by the congregation, came back to me as fresh as the morning dew:

> *On a hill far away stood an old rugged cross,*
> *the emblem of suffering and shame...*

While I was still at school, Father could not find any work. During the depression in the thirties he became one among thousands of the unemployed. My parents were quite religious and humble. Considering the great strain of everyday struggle, they were wonderful parents and looking back now I often wonder how on earth they managed. As for me, instead of paying attention to the teachers in school, I dreamed of finding some sort of paid work to help with the family finances. We lived in a terrace of ten houses, which are no longer there now. Our neighbours in that terrace were friendly and helpful in times of adversity. Two of my old neighbours remain my friends to this day.

I started work learning butchery with a Mr S. Ward, who was no relation to me. He insisted on cleanliness, punctuality and politeness to the customers. He did not suffer fools gladly, and taught me the trade well, giving me seven shillings and six pence for 60 hours of work a week. I learned how to cut up the meat, to make sausages and to keep the shop clean. With a bicycle, I delivered orders to customers. In April 1939 I joined the Territorial Army.

Then in August of that year the war loomed. On Friday, the 1st of September we were mobilized. At noon on Sunday, the 3rd of September, news came on the radio that we were at war with Germany. My division was stationed in Norfolk for twelve months before it was moved to Melrose in Scotland and later to Worcestershire, where we were on full war footing. In early October 1941 the embarkation began. How much we had taken our freedom and our well-sheltered life for granted while we were in Great Britain. But when we started to think of what we would be leaving behind, it was heart-rending. As for me, the loved ones included a girl I was courting while the division was stationed in Cheshire.

I remember the day we met so well. It was a Sunday in April 1941 while my colleague, Jim, and I were walking on the heath. We came upon a young girl (later we learned that she was seventeen) sitting on a bench. Girls were not my strong point in those days, but Jim said he wanted to have a go at her. While he did all the talking, I dreaded the thought that he was making a fool of such an innocent-looking girl. I had to devise a way of saving Elsie by making a date with her to tell her that Jim was a married man. In doing so I fell in love with her, and still love her dearly to this day.

Five months after my first meeting with Elsie, we were separated as the division went overseas. She worked as housekeeper to an elderly lady, Miss Ashworth, who encouraged her to join the St. John's Ambulance Brigade. For two years and a half after Singapore had fallen to the Japanese, Elsie and my parents and relatives had no news of my survival. Meanwhile she took up nursing in a large hospital in Salford, Manchester, and carried on as a nurse until her retirement.

I often recalled our parting at Norwich Station in October 1941. We said goodbye there and promised to love each other and marry when the war was over. It was to be four years and one month before we were to meet again.

There were heavy bombing raids on our towns and cities by the German Air Force. Great Yarmouth had been hard hit by constant raids.

We were told that our unit was to leave for Egypt from Liverpool. But after a long sea voyage via Canada, we changed to American troopships. The next day we put to sea again for Trinidad, then on to Cape Town, arriving at the time of the Japanese attack on Pearl Harbour, which brought the Americans into the war. We stayed 12 days in Cape Town. Whilst there we learned that our destination had been changed and the division was diverted to Bombay.

After three weeks in India we sailed for Singapore. Two days before arriving at that destination the convoy came under attack from 27 Japanese planes. Fortunately no ship was damaged, but there were many near misses. The escort ships protected us well with gunfire and we sailed safely through the Straits of Malacca.

The 18th Division landed in Singapore on the 29th of January 1942 but by then the Japanese had already reached Johore. The causeway was destroyed, cutting Singapore off from the mainland. The situation was hopeless. Singapore surrendered, and the cease-fire began at 4 p.m. on the 15th of February 1942. All troops were ordered to make their way to Changi where we began our lives as Prisoners of War.

We were put to work at Singapore dockyard in groups of twelve men or more to load cars, trucks, bicycles, oil drums, street light standards and trolley buses onto ships bound for Japan. We could only guess that the Japanese needed all that they could turn into metal at that time.

Our working parties consisted of the British and Australian soldiers kept in Changi Camp while civilians were interned in Changi Jail where some groups of soldiers were also put under heavy guard.

Conditions quickly deteriorated. The monotonous diet of rice, to which we were unaccustomed, began the rapid process of debilitation that lasted to the end of the war.

On the 19th of June 1942 our working parties were rounded up and put on a train, 31 men to a boxcar, with hardly any room for us to sit. Hence, each prisoner took turn to sit and to stand during the six-day journey to Baan Pong in Thailand where the Thailand-Burma Railway (which later became known as the Death Railway) was to start. I remember the day the train pulled in at Baan Pong so well. It was a day before my 21st birthday. At home in England there would surely be a celebration but that day was like all the other days we survived as PoWs under the Japanese, our captors. I told some of my fellow PoWs about it and I remember hearing 'What a way to spend one's 21st birthday' and nothing more.

My thoughts wandered to home and what my loved ones must be thinking since there was no news for them whether I was dead or alive. From memory, I visualized a train journey back to Great Yarmouth, passing large and small oak trees, hedgerows and fields. *No, today there will be no celebration,* I thought to myself. Life constantly under threat and brutality, sustained by meagre portions of rice and drops of water, was not worth a celebration.

But all the same I was glad to be alive still, with a hope though faint to a point of becoming hopeless, that I would be among those who would survive through thick and thin, the atrocities, the heartlessness, the enemies' swords, the beatings, malaria, cholera and starvation.

Baan Pong gave me a glimpse of the Thai people. Almost overnight, makeshift shacks sprang up near to our camp. Trading became brisk. We were able to barter pens, watches, and cigarette lighters for some food. Each day we were forced to march three kilometres to Non Pladuk. Here we cleared the land to build bamboo huts, our base camp, along the railway line. Later the area became a large railhead with workshops and go-downs and close to an ack-ack battery which gave us cause for concern as we were now crowded into a camp near to what was an important bombing target.

Our fear proved true later with tragic results. About 500 of us, who survived the bombardment, were kept in Non Pladuk until May 1943. Then our group was transported to a point where we had to go on foot. We were marched for three days to Kinsio, which was a sea of mud under the monsoon rain. It was here that the cholera epidemic struck. In the first month, more than 75 per cent of the PoWs suffered from cholera attack. The monsoon made the working conditions extremely difficult, washing away bridges and turning roads into rivers, and with it, a fresh outbreak of disease.

Food supplies could not reach us, and we were without medical aid, but without delay we were marched on again to Konkuta, a large camp three miles south of the Three Pagodas Pass, bordering Burma. The long march to Konkuta was deadly; every yard was a quagmire, and many of us could not keep up and so the Japanese beat us severely.

The track on which we walked was perilous, and some bridges were only partly constructed. Crossing them was like walking on a tightrope, being goaded on by the rifle butts of the guards. At night, any of us who slipped and fell off a bridge or could not go any farther would be left behind. At times we were allowed to stop at small camps along the way to eat some boiled rice and vegetables and drink tea. Thousands of Tamils, Chinese and Malay labourers had been moving north to work on the railway, and they too succumbed to the elements. We passed a number of bodies on the jungle tracks on the way.

By this time, most of the PoWs working on the Death Railway looked haggard, just skin and bones. Our clothing was a hotchpotch, ragged and mud-coloured, soaked most times with perspiration. New clothes were not available, and footwear did not last long. As a result, most of us were barefooted.

At Kinsio, cholera struck friends and foes alike. It was swift and merciless, spreading with a horrific speed. It was obvious that as each day went by the Japanese became more and more pressed to advance the railway to Burma. In so doing they became more brutal. The beating and the torture of the PoWs had been a routine.

From May 1943 onwards there developed on the construction of the railway the violent treatment of PoWs which occurred frequently to force us to make greater efforts. No matter how hard we worked it seemed less and less we met the work tasks laid down. Many times I helped to carry sick men on stretchers to the work site. But unable to stand, the sick lay there waiting to die either from the sword or from the disease. Those who could move or lift objects were continually beaten for being slow or for failing to understand instructions that were shouted at us in Japanese.

At times the enraged guards kicked us or struck us with with bamboo rods kept handy for that purpose, while Japanese officers used the flat of their swords. The beating was often followed by a specific punishment such as holding a rock above one's head while standing for hours on end. When we could no longer hold up the rock, or moved from the position, we received another beating for disobedience. The tortures of the PoWs were just something that the guards indulged in; it was a part of a disciplinary system in which the railway engineers and Japanese officers of the Prisoner of War Administration participated.

In most camps the daily routine began with roll-call followed by breakfast of boiled rice and tea, then we collected our working tools and by 8 a.m. we had to arrive on foot to work on the railway line twenty kilometres away. Walking such a distance every day was quite an ordeal since most of the PoWs had no shoes or any other form of footwear. Depending on the mood of the guards, we might get a break of about an hour. If the camp was near to the work site a meal of rice and dried vegetables or fish was brought out to the prisoners. After lunch we worked on until 4 p.m. Many a time we had to work through the night by the light of oil flares, without returning to the camp. Sometimes we could go back to the camp in the evening, completely exhausted. With luck we might be allowed to wash in the stream nearby.

In the evening there was another roll call. No lights were provided, so some chores had to be done by the light of camp fires or primitive lamps fuelled by palm oil which came our way by stealing or smuggling.

When some of us had some energy left or could not easily fall asleep, the talk of food dominated the conversation as most of us were so very hungry. In what little time we had for leisure it was very difficult to make friends owing to the daily struggle for survival. However, I believe that many PoWs formed lasting friendships, which during that time helped them to endure and survive. Otherwise, life and survival would have no meaning, especially with the Japanese intolerance and lack of any humanity or conscience.

To the Japanese, there was no difference between the British and the Dutch, between the Australian and the New Zealanders. To them we were the same, their slaves. In our camp at Konkuta there were mostly British and Australian PoWs. An Australian sergeant named Eddy was a good sport. I remember him well, and also will not forget an incident that took place when two sections of the railway line were joined by brass fish plates, which were missing the next morning. Rumours had it that the Aussies from our camp were responsible. It seemed they were experts at helping themselves to things that were lying around.

The Thailand-Burma railway required several bridges. The day I first set sight on the bridge on the Kwai, which has since been made famous by novels and films, it was being constructed. Each of its buttresses was clothed in scaffolding. Wanting to reach Burma as quickly as possible the Japanese had the first bridge built entirely of timber, two hundred yards in length, to get the track across until the concrete bridge was completed.

Finally the last railway line was laid with quite a ceremony, and on the 25th of October 1943 the line was opened to traffic, but not for long as the Allies soon had the news of its completion. The bombing of the railway and the bridges started with increasing intensity. At this stage the Japanese appeared to panic as things were going badly for them in Burma and elsewhere. They decided to move us back. Leaving Konkuta, we arrived at Hindato just before Christmas 1943. Here, the Japanese put us in working parties again to cut down trees, making wood piles at regular intervals along the railway line as fuel for steam locomotives.

In September 1944, we were moved to Non Pladuk where we built a new camp called Non Pladuk No.2, which was close to the old camp of 1942. In the night of the 6th of September, we were awakened by the sound of low-flying aircraft. Then the whole sky turned so bright that it was just like daylight. After the first aircraft dropped the flares the rest kept coming, one after another, dropping bombs until 7 a.m. The last bomber flew over our camp, evidently going for the railhead. The bombs fell short and straddled the two camps, killing 99 PoWs and injuring 330 others. The scene was of utter devastation. To be on the receiving end of our own planes was hard to bear. Non Pladuk was mostly destroyed. Later that week another air raid killed six more men.

Shortly afterwards, I joined a group of volunteers going up country to Konyu, working on the repair and maintenance of the railway. A new wave of air raids made the Japanese more panicky. As a result we were ordered to return to Non Pladuk. The sight that met us was sheer devastation. It seemed that a series of air raids had wiped out the entire camp. The PoWs had been moved to Bangkok.

Only a few Japanese and Korean guards remained, showing no interest whatsoever. While there, we witnessed the arrival of several trains that had managed to come through the line, carrying injured Japanese soldiers. Forgetting their brutality, inhumanity and all the atrocious acts they had committed, we tried to help, giving them some food and water.

We lived rough for several days in what remained of Non Pladuk before being moved to Bangkok. The journey proved to be very difficult. Badly damaged bridges delayed us. The bridge on the Kwai River had been under constant air attacks. In November 1944, it was so badly damaged that two spans fell into the river. So the Japanese tried to repair them and put into use the wooden bridge. However, it was destroyed on two occasions.

In May 1945, our group arrived in Bangkok and we were put on board a motor boat to go up the Chaopraya River to be interned in a large warehouse on a river bend. Once again, we were subject to air attacks as the area of the go-downs contained much of the Japanese equipment, hundreds of oil drums and stores. With no time to rest, we were quickly put into trucks to work in an area near to the Grand Palace, in a well-guarded storage compound. Inside, there were stacks of 50-gallon oil drums for us to sort out the full oil drums from the empty ones. Once, an air raid warning went off causing the Japanese guards to run for cover, leaving us to our own devices. So, with a fellow PoW, I went out and away from the oil drums and walked down the road, passing Thai houses along a canal. The local people also appeared to be in a state of panic, as we could by now hear the sound of a bomber approaching. A Thai couple standing in front of their house beckoned us to take shelter with them in the basement until it was safe. Though few words were spoken, and not knowing Thai, I could only sense that they were friendly and hospitable, making our brief contact a warm and heartfelt one.

In Bangkok, occasionally we came into contact with Thai people, some of whom gave us gifts and news. One man who spoke some English told me that soon the war would be over. Then one day the Japanese did not make us go out to work as usual but allowed us to go on to the quayside. When the Japanese whistles sounded to warn of another air raid we ran to a field down the road, and soon a formation of R.A.F. Liberator planes flew in and bombed the go-downs and the barges containing German-owned rubber in the nearby canal, setting them ablaze. When we could return to our quarters, we saw that the damage was enormous. I saw one dead PoW amid the clutter of debris.

After this bombing our unit was trucked to a railway station, and from there a train carried us to Ubol, bordering Lao and Cambodia in Esarn, the northeastern region of Thailand. Why the Japanese took us out of the capital to a far-flung Esarn province some 650 kilometres away, I could only guess. My anxiety was that we were to be left in an impoverished area to starve to death, having seen how poor and desolate were the villages and the land we passed through.

Our party arrived in Ubol on the 23rd of June 1945. This was to be our last camp in captivity. I turned 24 years old here on Esarn's barren soil.

In the new camp the Japanese left us alone most times and occasionally the guards came to count our number. I remember one occasion when some local people tried covertly to contact us. In poor English one Esarn man said that the war would soon be over, but it was not until the 15th of August 1945 that we sensed something was in the wind.

The following day the war ended but we were not officially told until a week later. That was when a senior British officer, Colonel Toosey, came to our camp from Nakorn Nayok to see us.

Supplies of food began to arrive, and I was asked to assist in setting up 'the mess' as this had been my army function. On the 16th of September 1945 we left Ubol by train for Bangkok. On the way when the train stopped at Korat Station, some of us left the carriage to stretch our legs. On the platform there were many people to welcome us. One middle-aged man, with a smile, said 'Sawasdi' to me and handed me a short note written in English. The message, which I have among my few treasures to this day, reads:

Welcome.
I was glad to hear your having succeeded
and pleased your returning home.
Please God help you forever.

From a branch of Chinese Anti Japanese
North Eastern Association

I could hardly believe that amidst all the horror and destruction, some people still thought of us.

On arriving in Bangkok, we were taken to Don Muang Airport where Lord Mountbatten, Supreme Commander of S.E.A.C. and his wife greeted us, telling us that we were to be flown to Rangoon by the R.A.F. Transport Command when an aircraft was available.

On the 26th of September we reached Rangoon and were taken to the 12th Indian Field Hospital for medical checks, and seven days later we were moved to a large transit camp, with an advance of pay which enabled us to purchase goods we had not seen for years.

On the 11th of October 1945 we boarded the troopship S.S. Orbita and sailed home via Colombo, Port Said, the Suez Canal and Gibraltar where we had a day on land, sight-seeing.

The PoWs on board the ship were from various regiments picked up from several camps in Thailand. The ship dropped anchor in Liverpool Bay late afternoon of the 9th of November 1945. Next day at noon, we entered Gladstone Dock where we disembarked aided by Pioneer Corps personnel who carried our kits for us. After refreshment we were taken by army trucks to Huyton Transit Camp for further medical checks and for uniforms, pay and travel warrants before catching our trains for home.

On the 11th of November, I was on the train heading for Great Yarmouth, leaving the horrific nightmare of the last four years behind. I had cabled Elsie to meet me in Liverpool on the 10th of November. At the time she was nursing in Hope Hospital in Salford, Manchester, thirty miles from Liverpool but she was on duty that day and unfortunately the matron would not permit her to change her day off with another nurse.

As the train sped towards Market Harborough I consoled myself. I thought 'Thank God I survived the tortures, the slavery, the devastating disease in the jungle of Thailand working on the Death Railway, so I should be able to wait a little longer to meet Elsie, who after all has been waiting all those years for me.'

At Market Harborough Station we learned that the train we were on was for London, but there would be seats for us on the Norwich train although we would have to wait for a few hours. On this journey with me was another former PoW. "I'm Ray Ward," was all I could say to him, who had shared perhaps equally the horrors that befell thousands of PoWs. And equally tongue-tied Sam Syder did not venture further than telling me his name and that he came from Norwich. I had not met him previously but it was good to have

his company. His taciturn front was well understood. It would not be any good to talk of the war, of the atrocities, the horrors and the dead in the jungle of Thailand right then and there. Sam seemed to have already stored deep inside his soul such painful memories, and I must not cause more pain to both of us, opening the wounds. Hence we, two laconic men recently landed on home-ground, hid deep inside each of us horrendous tales as we mingled among our own people.

Sam and I went window-shopping to spend time while waiting for our train. We could not buy anything as we had only been given ten pounds in Liverpool where we spent most of that amount. But then I sensed a warm, happy feeling slowly and softly enfolding me, like an eiderdown in a wintry night. Gently it wrapped me into its folds, this joy of home-coming, away, so far away now from my tormentors, hunger, slavery, sickness, the cries of men in pain and the fear of dying there in the jungle of Kanchanabury, in the west country of Thailand. For a brief moment I was not sure of the reality, afraid that it was only a dream of being home in England that I often had at Non Pladuk and Konkuta.

Finally I arrived at Great Yarmouth's Vauxhall Station where my sister Joyce and a friend of our family and Salvation Army bandsman, Sydney Gibbs, awaited me while my parents stayed at home to welcome me.

It happened so fast...the fuss my father and mother made on arrival. *Hold on to me now,* I wanted to say, *and never let me go anywhere so far from home ever again. Tell me this is not a dream.*

A few months later I was discharged from Northampton Demob Centre. Elsie spent Christmas 1945 with us, and we became engaged. We were married on the 16th of March 1946 and settled in Great Yarmouth. I had a job with the British Rail and Elsie became a warden in charge of sheltered accommodation for 32 elderly residents, a responsibility she shouldered right up to the end of 1972.

Throughout our married life, she had been my best friend as well. Without her now, I feel only half of me is alive. In old age, I dread the journey into the past but when I do, I cannot help but thank all those who made it possible for me to survive and be home to see my loved ones again.

The Gunman

Ignorance is a source of suffering

Now if I am paid a million to shoot a man, I will not do it, for I have already killed too many men. The last one I killed was a teacher whose name I knew from a newspaper two days after having shot him. A hired gunman may know absolutely nothing of his victims, or any reasons why he must shoot them. All I had were his photograph and address. The rest was quite easy – a few days of watching, checking his routine and where to wait for the moment to pull the trigger.

I knew from a popular Thai daily that he was a schoolteacher and that morning he was on his way from his house to lead a protest against the leasing of a forest reserve from the Department of Forestry by the wife of a very powerful politician. But I did not know for sure who wanted him dead. A professional killer is not paid directly by the persons who want to have someone murdered. The orders come from several levels of agents. Boxers have their promoters and managers, and so have we. And like boxers, we have different ranks and prices. If you want to get rid of a top judge, for instance, you don't hire a low-grade gunman like me. I am not even a trained sharpshooter; I am just a peasant turned gunman.

When I read of the dead teacher in the newspaper and found out that he wanted to lead his students and their parents to make a protest in order to safeguard the woods of the district in which they live, I felt sick inside for having killed him. I could neither eat nor sleep for several days. I lay awake in my hiding place thinking of him, a brave and idealistic schoolteacher who questioned: "How can an individual or a company obtain forest reserves and public land to turn them into private properties if not through bribery?" Unaware of death some paces away, he came towards me, thinking I was one of the people who would join him in the protest march. The death of that schoolteacher made me think of my own past, the path that led me to become a murderer for hire.

I was born in a village in Mahasarakam Province, where Naamsiaw River is our lifeline, keeping us and the buffaloes and cows alive in searing summer seasons. In my young days, I could say wholeheartedly that there were plenty of fish, shrimps, frogs and eels in the water and rice in the paddy-fields, a saying we learned in school. Now there are hardly any fish in Naam Siaw or rice in the paddies. It began when several powerful investors, many of whom were politicians, turned arable land into salt farming. Vast areas of *tongna* (rice fields) became *naklue* (salt fields).

The salt farmers brought up the brine from underneath the soil and spread it on the prepared salt beds to be evaporated by the sun. From these *naklue* some of the brackish water seeped through the mounds; moreover, the waste was let go into the nearby rice fields and canals. It did not take long. The soil of our rice fields became salty and the water in Naam Siaw was also brackish, and then we could not grow rice and the fish died. We, poor and ignorant peasants, did not know at the time why such huge areas of farm land must be made into salt farming. We did not know that underneath the soil of Esarn there were salt deposits from which, in summer, salt appeared on the surface, making the bare earth white and crusty. Later in a newspaper we read that these salt farms supplied the salt to factories to produce glass and certain chemicals.

One year in April, we rice farmers whose fields were badly damaged by salt water from the influential men's salt farms, walked to the Wapipatoom District Office to tell the officials of our grievance. The police rounded us up as if we were a herd of buffaloes. Most of us were battered with wooden clubs and with the butts of the policemen's guns. A lot of us were bleeding very badly and then we were thrown in jail without any medical treatment to our wounds.

When the fish in Naam Siaw died and we could not grow rice any more, we had to sell our land very cheaply to the people who wanted to enlarge their salt farms. With the cash from selling our land, I hired a utility van to take my wife and child and my old father to a new land in Pakam District, southern Burirum, where many Wapipatoom rice farmers had gone ahead of us to find new places to live. One of them was my uncle, who helped me find a part of the woods which some powerful people claimed to be theirs and I, like all of the new settlers in that part of the forest, became a tenant.

It took only a few days to build a shack from hand-hewn trees and bamboo and corgon grass, and we started cutting down trees to burn, clearing the plot for planting maize and fruit trees. My father, my wife and I worked all day long to slash and burn and soon the forest land was bare and we waited for the rain to fall.

After a few monsoon seasons, news came that that part of Dongyai (big forest) and Naampud (Spring) Forest had been declared 'degraded' by the Department of Forestry due to us, squatters, who had encroached on the forest reserve. Therefore we must move out so that the so-called *degraded* forest could be given to concessionaires to plant commercial trees, the eucalyptus trees, in the name of reforestation. Armed men came and cut down fruit trees and burned the shanties and arrested most of the squatters, but my family and I, not knowing where we could move on to, stayed on while we were not bodily pushed out of our new home. I happened to hear from my neighbours that in nearby Naampud Forest there was a conservationist monk with a group of his followers, who were trying to protect the woods from being logged and turned into eucalyptus plantations. The priest, Pra Prajak, and the fearless laymen tried to protect the trees in the sanctuary by keeping watch and by 'ordaining' each big tree. They tied yellow robes around the trees to ordain them and thus make them sacred against the chainsaws of loggers, but to no avail. Pra Prajak and many of his men were arrested and charged with encroaching on a forest and put in prison. Not long after the arrest of the monk and men, Naampud Forest was no more. Now you might see the eucalyptus trees thriving abundantly there as a source of supply to the pulp and paper factories. At the time no one talked about the harm to the soil and the environment eucalyptus trees could cause. This type of tree was chosen because it is the fastest growing tree, from which the investors could harvest their return in less than five years.

Meanwhile, without a new place to which we could move coupled with my father's illness, we remained on the land. One day armed men came while I was deep in the jungle in search of medicinal trees and herbs to cure my father. On my return I found that my shack was burnt and my wife and son and father were murdered. So, with unquenchable sorrow and fiery anger in my heart, I vowed revenge. I could shoot anyone I was paid to kill. But when I killed the teacher, who was trying to protect a forest reserve, I felt as if I had killed myself because at one time I had also tried to help Pra Prajak to safeguard Naampud.

The men who killed my wife and my son and my father and several settlers of Dongyai and Naampud were hunting me because

I survived and knew of their evil deeds. I escaped by walking a long distance to avoid all the police checkpoints at Suengsang, Konbury, Chokechai and Paktongchai. I did not feel safe even when I was on a bus heading south to Kabinbury and eventually to Bangkok.

In Bangkok, I was too old to be a boxer and too illiterate to be anything but a labourer, carrying sacks of rice at a large silo on the bank of Chaopraya River. There, I got mixed up with some dubious characters. One of them was a hitman in hiding after having done a kill. To me, he boasted about a contract on a business tycoon who had survived several attempts by other professional murderers. We took to each other as if we were brothers, being Esarn men. When he showed me his pistol, the tool of his trade, I trembled, holding it in my hand. My heart beat fast as I aimed it at several images of my family's murderers. To kill them I must know how to use the gun, and my big brother from Chaiyapoom taught me well.

In a span of five years I killed twenty-nine men and one woman, and in the trade I quickly became known as *muepuensamsipsop* (the thirty-corpse gunman). As a result, I could command a high price per head. But among the professionals, I was still classed as low grade because I lacked finesse and certain techniques of following and shooting. Those big brothers said I rushed in, eager to pull the trigger. True enough, I did not care for finesse and the risk of having witnesses or leaving traces behind. The main thing was that I wanted to kill, though I did not know whether the targets were good or bad, honest or greedy, labour leaders or highly corrupt and manipulative politicians, environmental activists or grabbing land speculators. I hoped that some of the dead might be those responsible for destroying rice fields and rivers with waste from salt farms and factories and for evicting poor people from their homes to make way for dam constructions or eucalyptus plantations, and for logging and destroying forest reserves and national parks.

When I was paid to kill a young man in Khon Kaen, I was reluctant, having just taken the life of the far-sighted and fearless schoolteacher. I delayed the shooting for a week because this time I wanted to know a little of the man I was to murder. At least I wanted to know his name and his profession instead of having his photograph and address in my pocket. It would be easy to silent a man of no importance, of no power and protection. Asking quietly about him I knew that he was a student who was leading a protest against the pollution of the Pong River and the Chee River by factories on their banks and salt farming in Mahasarkarm, my own province. Should I end the life of a young man who was doing the very thing I should have done myself, had I only known how? The Pong River and the Shee River are lifelines of millions of people in Esarn. But then they have been so badly polluted with waste from the pulp and paper mills, sugar factories and tapioca flour factories that millions of stinking dead fish floated along the route of more than 300 kilometres from Khon Kaen to Ubol. The polluted water became useless. As a student, he must have known the untold damage the pollution had caused to rivers and rice fields.

I went to him and told him of the plot to do away with him, and then I crossed the Mekong River and lived quietly in Lao, changed my identity and became a monk for three months, residing in a temple of Luang Prabang. I will not return to Esarn. Here in Lao we speak the same language; the Laotians and the people of Esarn are closely linked through cultural heritage and language. I might have wanted to go back to Esarn if my father, my wife and my son were still alive, despite the fear that one day the Big Boss of hired gunmen would order another assassin to kill me for not accomplishing the job assigned and for knowing too much.

Because in those days I was a poor and stupid peasant of Esarn, who could barely read and write, it took me years to know that as tenants of powerful people who claimed forest reserves as their own, we were their instruments to slash and burn the trees, big and small, so that a few years later the woods could be classified as 'degraded'. And because of rampant corruption all along the way, in high places and well as low, the so-called *pa sium soam* (deteriorated forest) and parts of national parks fell into the hands of property developers, golf course owners, and eucalyptus planters. It took me years to realize why brave and idealistic men like Nid Chaiwana, the teacher of Baan Huaykaew School in Chiangmai and that student of Khon Kaen University must be removed. And I was one of the many instruments which brought death to so many good men, men who fought against evil.

Here, in Lao, I now see what is happening to the Lao forests that loggers have been eyeing with sheer greed. Now the Australian government-sponsored bridge across the Mekong River has been finished, making the transportation between Thailand and Lao faster and easier, it will not take long for them to rob Lao of her trees, leaving the denuded hills and eroded land behind.

A Rare Thai

Incorruptible but not invincible

I met a lovely girl at a rugby match. Among a group of her girlfriends, she stood out so remarkably that I wished to know her. At the time we were both students – she was in her final year at Triam Udom High School and I was ambitiously trying to be the first in my class to attend the Military Academy.

In the Academy, I sometimes took second or third, but mostly I came out on top and my name has been engraved on gold plaques as a result. I never once played truant. As a good all-rounder both in the academic performances and in behaviour, I collected prizes and praises. But sports have never been my strong point.

Gradually Siriluck and I became good friends, and eventually she changed her mind. She had intended to maintain celibacy for the rest of her life, being a very strict Buddhist. Still she asked me to practise the *silas* or precepts set by the Lord Buddha. Hence, I stopped smoking, drinking alcoholic beverages and smoking. We made a vow that we would not waste our time watching films, shows and all forms of entertainment. The time saved was spent on our studies.

In the Fifth Grade of the Military Academy I was appointed the Leader, honoured as the Representative to appear at functions outside on various occasions. Responsibilities were increased, and I became outstanding, too outstanding perhaps. But, at the time, I was not aware of its adverse effect. How little did I know that being too outstanding and doing good deeds to benefit others could put one in somebody's way or arouse envy and malice. All that time some people went about secretly trying to find fault.

When I organized a film show to raise funds for the Academy, it was considered wrong. Therefore, punishment was rendered. I could not receive my sword upon graduation until three months later after other graduates received theirs. The rank of the Leader was stripped from me and I was placed on the bottom rung of the honour list. That was the first time I was aware of how one could lose honour at the wave of a hand. What are honour and position and name when a mere stranger or an adversary could take them away with the wave of a hand?

When Siriluck and I were married, we tried to save for a house, and I sought extra income from teaching in my spare time. Then I won an award to study in a military academy overseas. Upon my return to Thailand I entered the monkhood, following a tradition more than anything.

My mother-in-law has been much concerned with her daughter's well-being. She believes that 'wives of military personnel count bottles while wives of policemen count bank notes'. True, I did not have enough money to buy a car. To own a second-hand car, my wife had to sell her diamond ring. And since then she has not had a desire to wear a ring. But we loved this old car so much that when it was out of order, we felt as if our loved one was ill. When it was scratched, we suffered as if we were damaged. This showed that I too suffered all that time from the power of possession, of attachment to material things.

As a major general I had been allocated an accommodation by the government for a year until someone high up considered that we were too comfortable. So there was an order for us to move out. The move coincided with my plan to leave inner Bangkok for suburban life and the area my wife and I chose was Ladprow. At that time Ladprow was mainly rice fields. We built our cottage and lived without electricity and water supply.

For three years we lived there. We had kerosene lamps for light and we bathed in a pond. We took delight in watching sunrise and sunset each day. It was tough, living a frugal and spartan life. My wife never complained, not even once. I took pity on her, and borrowed money from a bank to build a more decent house despite the fact that it would take me years and years to repay the loan. Fortunately we did not have children while we were trying to accumulate things the society expected us to have.

How lost we were then, wallowing in the mire of craving. How we took pride in having a car, a house and land, not realizing that we were travelling in a different direction from that of Lord Buddha.

As I moved up the hierarchy, I began to see that I was more lost, devoting too much of my time to worldly pleasures. At this point we began our quest to find our way back, seeking out famous abbots or the widely acclaimed monks in various temples in and outside Bangkok, only to be aware later that in so doing we had taken another wrong turn. But instead of turning away completely from famous monks, we still go to the Wat and try to find our way back to Lord Buddha and follow strictly his teaching. In time we increased our observation of the *silas* from the Five Precepts to the Ten Precepts. To follow assiduously the Ten Precepts, we rid ourselves of most worldly materials including our personal belongings. We also got rid of the land, the house, the furniture and the car, and built a simple little hut near a temple. We lived there with bare necessities. There is only a stubby little desk crudely made for me to write notes and letters, sitting on the floor to do it. There was no need for a chair or a table or a bed.

These days we sleep on the hard wooden floor so as to rid ourselves of the attachment to comfort. I eat one vegetarian meal a day at noon to be frugal as well as to decrease the expenses on food. This practice is also a part of the observation of the Ten Precepts. The vegetarian dish is prepared at home and then consumed at the office.

Earlier on both my wife and I gave up our bank accounts in which we had accumulated some money in the past. We agreed not to gather and hoard anything, including cash so there was no need to have a bank account.

Following closely the teaching of the Lord Buddha, I can see things clearly as they are, though by now some people consider that I have become a crank because of the observation of the Ten Precepts and frugality. Some hold doubts and suspicion, and many have come out openly to attack me. But then, to me and my wife, praise, flattery, honour, rank, a sense of grandeur, gossip, and attacks have no effect on us. For all along both of us have already decreased greed, lust and anger to a considerable extent. The strict observation of the Ten Precepts can also make one diligent, not lazy, and one becomes less selfish and corrupt.

Once a construction company tried to bribe me with millions of baht so that I would put its project on top priority for the Prime Minister to pass, but I declined the offer. This company wanted to jump the queue. In so doing, it would not have to pay a huge sum of money in interest.

Yes, I have been well aware that my position at Government House is but transitory. In the morning I walk up the steps to my office and in the evening I walk down. I have been criticized for being too strict, too honest, too straightforward, too righteous and too much of a good Buddhist. It has also been said that such a powerful position should never have been given to a person like me.

On the contrary, I believe that the higher the positions, the more controlled and honest and incorruptible one should be. If you were me, would you accept the millions offered to push a construction project forward? Would you help a certain telecommunications company to obtain a monopoly? Would you assist several private concerns to have concessions to mine, to log, to turn forest reserves into eucalyptus plantations?

Why would I want millions of baht offered to me as a bribe when I, of my own volition, have given up two meals a day, closed all our bank accounts and got rid of our house? My wife and I are now homeless, living under the roof of a Buddhist temple. For this is our ultimate goal of the liberation from greed, lustful desire and temperament, according to Lord Buddha's way to the cessation of craving and suffering.

Siriluck and I are very much at peace now in both religious and worldly sense. There is a constant flow of 'santi' (peace) and calm joy within us, despite the awareness that some very powerful people want to *dong* (pickle) me to get me out of the way.

Two Soka Boys

A destiny worse than death

"**W**hat are they doing?" Danprai asked Kumpan, who was still panting because they had been running along the hot sandy path. Dan wanted to repeat the question, but then Kum sat down on his heels. Dan squatted too, next to his friend. Their elbows touched. But the meagre shade of the tamarind tree could not give them any comfort. Kum's serious looks and silence compelled Dan to be quiet. Yet he would not take his eyes off Kum while the perplexity of *why are they doing that* recurred in his mind so that he had to inquire. When there was no answer, Dan turned to the congregation of yellow-robed monks and solemn old men and grey-headed women, sitting on the bare ground in the glare of the sun. The priests, hands cupped in the manner of praying, had been chanting in unison one magical mantra after another.

Why must they perform such a rite in the horribly hot sun? Dan wanted to ask but dared not speak. In front of the spellbound crowd was a toad tied to a stake. Terrified by the human din, the exposure and the fiery heat, it was trying in vain to free itself. The curious boy's eyebrows curved into another silent question. Shifting uncomfortably, he searched Kumpan's face for explanation once more. The friend remained stern and silent.

"Why?" Dan dared to utter at the risk of breaking the spell, nudging Kumpan with his elbow.

The older boy made a low grunting sound and then lapsed into silence again, staring intently at the monks and laymen and grandmothers as if to immerse himself in the awesome ritual.

Dan's grandmother and Kum's were among the people who had been submitting themselves to the cruel sun along with the terrified toad and the rest of the people gathered there. Missing were the schoolteacher, a modern man who did not believe in such a rite and Jek Jia, the Chinese shopkeeper. The latter had already packed up his goods and moved elsewhere since there was no more money to be made from the penurious, drought-stricken peasants of Soka, the forgotten community on the Plain of Nadhone.

We couldn't walk barefoot on the simmering sand today, Dan wanted to say. *We had to skip and run. Why do the grown-ups make themselves so pitiful?* The boy was very much moved by the sight of his grandmother while she swayed her perspiring, emaciated frame to the rhythm of helplessness. Dan recalled what Granny had said to the members of the Poontawi family, that if the monsoon did not come soon, it would mean famine. Her prediction fell on all ears. Her fearful word 'famine' dampened any hope that could be had from a cloud in the heavens. Tongue-tied, nobody could comment on or acknowledge her despair. The wizened woman lamented further, mumbling that in all her life there had never been a drought as severe and depleting as this.

The hellish wind rose from the seared plain, bringing with it swirls of dust and dry leaves. Huaysai, the creek that took the water out of distant Srisurachwood, had become parched. Though bores had been dug in various parts of its bed, there was no moisture in the hard clay. On the contrary, there seemed to be mockery from the Lord of Darkness on the dignity and significance of mankind. What could the people of Soka and of many hamlets subject to the curse do? They must torment themselves so that divinity above would take pity on the tied toad and human beings who had silently endured three successive years of drought.

The rain-begging rite was their last hope when human resources failed. But Dan, being only twelve years old, did not understand the meaning of it. Nevertheless, he had been taught to respect the solemnity of the monks and the old people. He sensed the utter despair prevailing in the burning air.

As if he could not bear the rite any longer, Kum gave up his serious pose. Taking Dan by the hand to lead the way, he forged forward over the hot sand, still in awe and silence.

Hunger drove them from the desolate hamlet into a copse to hunt for lizards. When they had caught three of these skinny reptiles, Kum made a fire and cooked their catch. After the scant meal had been wordlessly eaten, the fearful one seemed to have discarded his self-imposed silence while heat waves rose from the plain of salty earth and grey scrub and endless mirages. He coughed the dust out of his parched throat.

Then the two boys chose a wilting native gum tree. After a while the pensive boy could speak: "They tried to beg for rain from the Divine Lords."

"Will it rain then" Dan asked with a glint of hope.

"It might," Kum answered ruefully.

Dan scanned the skies for clouds and said hopefully: "Maybe in the evening, eh?"

Being without guile, it was a sincere attempt to comfort his laconic friend, who suddenly looked serious again, and stared at the grey infinity that was being distorted by the heat haze. Kum did not seem to mind the flies covering the wound on his left knee.

"The drought might be so bad that we won't have to go to school, Dan ventured to add after a long pause.

Could Kumpan Meesap be comforted? Not having to attend the distant primary school in Baan Nadhone under the gruelling supervision of the teacher who had a habit of flogging the children? So Dan's idea of walking fourteen kilometres daily to Nadhone Primary to learn under the cruel teacher seemed more frightening than the famine.

"It's bad enough now," Kum groaned. "We've nothing to eat and my father is going to sell me."

Instantly Dan became mute. The thought that his friend would be taken away from Soka by a broker to the capital so far away sent fear deep into his heart, for he could also be sold like several boys and girls ahead of him. The agent lived only fifty kilometres away in Nachuk. But despite that dread, Dan dared to say: "You can come to live with us."

But both boys knew that was not to be. Thus Kum confirmed: "My father will definitely sell me. The agent has been to see him." After having swallowing, the frightened boy admitted a shameful fact: "He also asked me to undress."

"No!" Dan cried. "Not that!"

"Yes."

"Did he touch you?"

"He had a good look at me..."

The youngsters knew very little of the criteria that particular branch of commerce use for terms of agreement and pricing. But the two Soka boys left it at that, having touched on the gate of their despair.

Days passed but no rain came. There was not even a faint rumble of thunder or the sight of rain-bearing clouds to raise hope. Meanwhile, several families left the village for elsewhere, where ponds and streams and rivers held water most of the year and where the monsoon was regular and the earth yielded. Rumours of those going to leave next spread fast; the straggling band of inhabitants called out their goodbyes. Ox-carts laden with sad-eyed peasants and their children and possessions rolled away, leaving dust and memories behind. Soka mourned its departing people. Despair tinged the sounds of goodbye. In parting, the two sides reminded one another of centuries of filial ties and kinship. The trembling voices of the aged sang back across the gulf of hopelessness. They wailed: "Will we ever see you again?"

Meanwhile, the adults talked of more rites and sacrifices to gain mercy from the Rulers of the Earth and the Sky. For rain, life and the normal turn of the season. Dan would rather suffer in place of his grandmother or of most of the old men and women, for he felt so utterly sorry for them. Perhaps they might let him join in some of the ritual and make him a sacrifice. His suffering might help them succeed and so prevent Kum from being sold.

Dan had not been included in all of the adults' doings, and they completely ignored him. Being a mere boy, he could only watch silently how the men killed a pig for the blood and flesh as votive offerings to the spirits at the village spirit house.

The rain-begging rites looked more macabre as seen through the eyes of the boy, who believed that the Soka men had become frighteningly desperate. The fatal twist of the knives, the mortal wounds, the deadly cries of the sacrificial animal, and the flow of blood pointed to one thing: the men were slipping backward towards primeval savagery and cruelty. The ancient bitterness and hatred, passed on from heart to heart since the brutal centuries of slavery to construct the mini Angkor at Pimai, had found vent in an acceptable form.

One day, Dan went off by himself into the heart of the Plain of Nadhone; the vastness of the arid landscape made the tiny boy more minute and singular. Without Kum by his side, he began to be afraid of the solitude and the great expanse. He halted several times to turn and look back towards Soka.

Where Dan chose to sit was unprotected by any vegetation. Sitting cross-legged under the excruciating sun, he closed his eyes and tried to pray, but since he had not been taught the art, his was only an imitation of the ways of monks and village elders he had observed. He swayed his head a little the way his Grandmother did, seeing her now in his mind's eye.

"Pity me, O Spirits," Dan prayed.

The experience was both enthralling and fearful. For he dared to be in the forefront so as to catch the eye of the ultimate power. The sheer silence of Nadhone weighed heavily on him. The sun whipped him so mercilessly that his head throbbed painfully, and what liquid there was in him became perspiration that was dripping down his face and torso.

"Pity me, O Lords," Dan chanted in the manner of the monks.

Gradually, courage came to him and helped him to expand. Departing from himself, he saw the image of Kum being taken away from Soka by the hideous agent. Dan silently asked: "Must it come to this? When will it be my turn?"

He saw himself and his friend leaving the plain for home, hallooing and laughing, riding their buffaloes in one of the good years. Then a recollection of Grandmother merged in. It was a picture of happiness when Granny turned to smile broadly while harrowing a ploughed paddy. Old as she was, she worked unabatedly, provided that there was water enough to grow rice.

"O, my Lords, have pity on Granny. Please be merciful to her for I'm your sacrifice," Dan raised his voice.

The blazing sun continued to beat him hard, increasing the torture as if to test the boy's capability to endure. Dan prayed: "Lords, have mercy on Granny and on all the old people. Granny has nothing to eat; she is so old and bony. Have pity on the starving old people for they cannot dig for yams and taro or chase grasshoppers and catch lizards for food."

His endurance had its limit. Curiosity made him open his eyes to see the effect of his rite. But to his dismay the skies remained cloudless. There was no cool breeze to herald the coming of the rain. Heavy with disappointment, Dan sighed and shifted. Perhaps his suffering was seen as a child's play, a mockery of the solemn and sacred rituals reserved for priests and religious old men.

"O, powerful spirits, the true rulers of the earth," the heavy-hearted boy made another attempt, but no more words came. The heat from the glaring sun was immense. He trembled at the thought that he would be punished for his fanciful action. There seemed to be so much of the cynicism in life, the universal suffering, sorrow, the primeval cruelty and the futility of all things that the boy could not grasp. But then it was his own seriousness that frightened him so that he shuddered. There was no way out now except to prove his sacrifice to the Lords or else, he feared, he would be sold.

The knife taken from his father's toolbox flashed in the pitiless sun. Only then was he convinced that he would not fail, for the sacrifice would be so great that the Rulers of the Earth and the Sky would take pity on him and so yield rains. But the sharp metal opened the wound deeper than intended on his wrist. Dan winced with pain, throwing the instrument away. The flow of blood mortified him. Still he lifted the wounded hand towards the sun for the Lords to see till he fell.

Lying flat on his back, Dan tried to call out for help but could not. His throat was dry, and he trembled, seeing that darkness was descending quickly on him. Yet he hopefully concentrated on hearing any rumble of thunder that would mean rain.

An Impersonator

A 'kratoey' speaks

I was born in a village 30 kilometres from Muang Kalasin, Esarn, a male by birth, if not by nature. Girls in the village accepted me as one of them and the rest called me *katoey*... Mana the *katoey*. Such has been my identity. One thing I would not do is to have a sex change for I want to keep everything with which I was born, and has grown along with me. As you can see I have not added anything. Being a flat-chested impersonator does not impose any problem. A lot of *girls* have had their sex change, including the hormone treatment and silicone implants. Everything you see on little me is real, including my own hair.

I can be the fabulous Marlene Dietrich and the glamourous Marilyn Monroe, but Liza Minnelli and Shirley Bassey are more me – dark, vivacious, expressive. My favourite numbers are Bassey's *This is My Life, Big Spender and Some Day*. Minnelli's *Cabaret* has become boring; it has been flogged to death.

I am also good at using cosmetics and I adore perfume. Things I regret are my Adam's apple and noticeable veins on my hands and too big a *thing*, which is useless and proves cumbersome and a disadvantage when one wears tight fitting costumes. As for my male voice, I have, through the years, tuned it to sound slightly husky and sexy. Don't you think I'm sexy, darling?

You are not quite with it, are you? You should have laughed or at least smiled just now if you recognized whom I was impersonating. But you have seen me on stage of course. That was why you made a beeline for me, wasn't it? No, I never for one moment consider I am a man. Given a choice...as if the Big G up there does give each of us any choice. I would still choose to be what I have become. Life is not so dull this way. Of course, you cannot go flapping your wrists gaily all your life. You grow older each day, and there is nothing more pathetic than a bitter, bitchy ageing Oriental gay like the one you and I know. That is why I had to do something. Before that I drifted from one gay bar to another in search of someone to love and to love me. Night after night I spent in those bars, in the gay discos, prancing on the dance floor, but to no avail. Who would love this queer who has long passed a sell-by-date?

In those places, you appeared as a caricature of a prima donna, screaming, flapping the wrists, calling out 'bitch', 'ducky' or 'darling' in a croaky loud voice. Even then I knew it was only a schoolgirl's daydream to look for love of a man. When I was 28, I returned to Germany, no longer as a kept boy, a prostitute. From my savings, I studied hairstyling and stayed a long time in Europe as a hairstylist. While in Hamburg, I went into a night club where there had been female impersonation shows, known in the trade as drag shows. Dear me, that kind of act has been deep in my heart's desire! It must be wonderful to dress glitteringly, daringly, with strings of pearls around the neck, swishing and swinging a long pearl necklace or ostrich feather! So I frequented the club and got to know some of the *girls*. I had to push hard to have a part in the show, doing something close to home like the jazzy 'Madame Butterfly'. Eventually I became a long-lasting part of the show, and shared a pad with Christa (formerly Christian), a true blond transvestite who has a pair of boobs which would make a flat-chested woman burn with envy. We lived in Hamburg together like two lovely sisters, without that scheming Cinderella and her Prince Charming. It was a scream when Christa and I, for the hell of it, dressed up ravishingly, out for a kill.

If you ask that question again, I shall hit you hard. You must think it is clever to ask whether one is passive or active. And do not be condescending either. I do not need sympathy or pity. Contempt I do not mind, but pity, no. I am what I am and proud of it. I have become far more artistic, creative, sensitive and imaginative than a lot of dull beer drinkers and fat slobs, living off social welfare, or callous, stuffy men shuffling in and out of their offices and factories, or boring married couples who live mundanely in soul-destroying marriage ruts. These are exactly the people who look at me with contempt.

In Europe I have been living quite an exciting life. At least I do not put my head in the sand or be blind to what is going on around one, or go through life only to pursue the pleasures of eating and sex. After all, I speak and write German, read *Die Welt, Frankfurter Allegmeine* and discuss politics, the refugee problems, racial conflicts and the rise of the Neo-Nazi. In Thailand, you wallow in the quagmire of greed. Some extremely rich families make Ferdinand and Imelda Marcos of the Philippines look like children in kindergarten. They have a knack of transferring their assets around and abroad and hide their great wealth under the names of their servants, drivers and security officers when they do not want to overload their wives and children. Meanwhile there are millions of poor Thais trying to make ends meet, begging in streets, living under bridges or in some Buddhist temples among stray dogs. Thousands of young men and women offer themselves to be abused at bars, nightclubs, massage parlours, whoring beer gardens. Many sell their children to sweat shops and brothel operators.

If you want to know, I can tell you this much – my parents sold me to an agent of a brothel owner in Bangkok. I, at the age of 13, became a child prostitute so that my people could earn 20,000 baht, a mere 800 US dollars. But to them, poor debt-ridden peasants of Esarn, it meant getting out of debt and perhaps survival for a month or two. They can sell their children as unfeelingly as they did their buffaloes. As for me, they were probably so ashamed of me for being *katoey* that selling me was to be rid of that shame. Do you know what it was like to be sold and to exist for years in a brothel? Do you want to live a life of a sex slave among dozens of 12-13-14 years old sold boys to provide sexual services to men who are as old as one's father or grandfathers?

The customers looked at us boys with gleams in their eyes, licking their lips, pointing their fingers at the ones they wanted. Many a time I was taken to the men's cars or to some short-time hotels where the customers were waiting. There were some men who preferred to make a *rendez-vous* with my 'uncle' and me at a Silom Street corner where that famous fast food chain is now or at Lumpini Park at the Wireless-Rama 4-Sathorn intersection as they made kerb calling. Being quite popular due to my very young age and the well-endowed equipment, I was frequently booked to visit rich customers living in luxurious houses and condotels in Pattaya. On such journeys, my minder acted as my father and I his son to pass the guards on duty. The minder would speak quite loudly while the security men looked on us: "Son, you must behave now. We're visiting a very important friend of mine." Yes, I do remember well most of my clients, even those with whom I had only short sessions. Most of them were nice and kind; many were fat and fatherly; several were completely bald; and some were repulsively huge and hairy. You know, I often saw pictures of a great number of the past customers in pages of certain newspapers. You would not believe that many of them were very important and much respected personalities in society. Do you mind if I do not go into lurid details about what they did to me or I to them? You might not be able to stomach it.

When we boys started to have pubic hair and hair on our legs, the 'uncles' carefully shaved us so that the customers would not have any suspicion. Then I turned 16. All the shaving in the world would not help. I became less popular, obviously too old for most regular customers. So I was duly removed, and farmed out to a popular gay bar as a naked dancer and sex actor twice a night; the first one at 10.30 and the last at 0.30 hours. During the shows I must look as if I truly enjoyed being a sex object to a muscular performer for half an hour each show. Several years later I was given a job of a waiter, for I had passed the use-by-date of twenty. After that I could go out freely to walk the streets or to loiter at a certain shopping centre, and that was where I met my man from Germany – a cuddly bear he was, twice my age and thrice my weight! He was my prize won on my own without the set-up of a brothel or a gay bar – a respectable airline executive he is too. He wanted a relationship, not a short time interlude, and perhaps he wanted a poor young man to whom he could give the affection and care which he did not have from his parents during the war years, I surmised. After several visits to Bangkok, he decided to take me to Germany to live with him. That was the beginning of my European life.

It is boring to talk of loneliness, don't you think? Each of us is lonely in our own way. A happily married man who has a doting wife and adorable children may have a touch of it from time to time. I shall not complain about my life. Fate has a lot to do with it. Oh well, getting old too has a hand in it as well. Would you believe after reaching 25 I grew out of my cuddly bear's age group. He returned to Bangkok to find a younger thing to replace me!

Now, it is no longer my search for love. My love is for my audience. I like crowded bars; the noise and the mingling of human bodies are comforting. After our show was over, Christa and I, or sometimes I alone dropped into The Pit or Rudi's on the other side of the street for a drink or two to be a part of the normal gays. I sat quietly sipping my drink, looking at or listening to people around me, feeling relaxed, knowing that one was not there to pick up or to be had by anyone. I always wanted to come back to Thailand despite the fact that the minimum wage per day for Bangkok is less than four

US dollars, that there are quite a number of big crooks, gambling den operators, drug traffickers, petrol smugglers, bribe takers, vote-buyers, extortionists, and paedophiles in high places. They carry on, doing crooked deals to attain great wealth and power. I keep in mind that thousands of Thais have been massacred in the streets and that desperate peasants sell their children to brothel operators and sweat shop owners to survive. But, at the time, I was not quite ready to leave Germany. I wanted to make my first million first. When I returned, I had enough money to buy 40-50 boys from poor peasants of Esarn at the rate of 30,000 baht per boy. Then I gave all the bought boys back to their parents to whom I said: "Whatever happens, don't sell them again for now they are my sons. I have asked them to stay with you and work for you and look after you until you die!"

Two Esarn Brothers

A case of diverging lives

My dear brother,

We have just begun harvesting. Everyone is in the fields. At a time like this I miss you very much. We often talk about you. It is a pity that Mother cannot read and write. Now and again she asks somebody else to read your letters to her. She believes that I tend to hold back the real account, particularly the parts that tell of your problems and illness. She wants to suffer along with you and she cannot accept that you must face all the difficulties and troubles alone in strange places and among foreigners who are so different.

You know she did not want you to go away at all. Now in her old age she suffers, waiting for the day to see you come back to live here. She does not sleep well, and often tells us that she has had some terrible dreams. I have tried to understand why you have left us. I do not want to think that it is because you dislike toiling on the land. You always say in your letters that you miss us and think of our hamlet and our herd of buffaloes. This gives me a hope that one day you will come back and help me with the tasks in the fields and at home. The land, the home and the herd need you, and I need your help most of all.

Some months ago, Etan, our oldest buffalo, gave us another calf, an albino male, which we named Aidon. And now Etan is dead. When you and I were small we used to ride on her back together and make her run through water in that shallow stream near our fishpond, remember? She was the one on which you learnt to ride. She pulled the plough and the harrow over the years till her neck became hardened and finally broken. We worked her so heard till she died! May she be reborn as a human of high birth and in wealth and good health and so be happy and content throughout. Father keeps her long horns in our rice barn as a token of good luck. Etan has given me an insight into the duty of each life. When we are born, men or animals, we have our duty to our kind. Those docile buffaloes, though they are whipped and worked and eventually slaughtered for meat, never revolt. They give their service in silence and with endurance. When they die, they leave their hide and horns for men to use. Thus, life has meaning: living to serve.

Mine is a son's duty. I may live long yet, and endure hardship, illness and poverty to take care of our parents, respecting them, seeing to their needs. I listen to them and obediently follow their advice and tradition. It is my gratitude.

Time and again you write about your 'goal', your intention to be highly educated, your magnificent future, just like the teacher of Napo Primary School, Kroo Kumjui, who talks a great deal about graft, injustice, exploitation, changes and what he called 'the agent of change'. Fortunately our daily existence is still endurable, though we do not have money. Should I be ashamed because some people say we are stupid, poverty-stricken, downtrodden and buffalo-like? I know for a fact that the traders, buyers and shopkeepers treat me as if I were an idiot, cheating me through their weighing machines and often short-changing me. They suppress the price of our produce and swindle us at every turn so that it is not worth selling anything to them.

I do not hope to get much out of the wonderful promises of the masters and the politicians. I do not fret when there are a lot of people growing richer from our labour, paying so little when they hire us and when they buy our produce, but then they sell their goods to us at high prices. Like Father and Mother, I believe in the force of karma and in silent endurance. Our parents have passed on to me their beliefs in non-violence and humility. It is not our way to whinge, to air our grievances and to haggle for higher pay from the merchants at each sale. Like father, I accept what is given. Though they may rob me through price suppression and cheat me with the weighing machines and in accounting, I utter not a word. I can still face hardship in the rice fields. I can look other men in the eye and say: 'I have never cheated anyone, robbed anyone, have not done harm to anyone, have not stabbed anyone in the back, have not trampled over anybody to get what I want'. No, they cannot plunder what I have accumulated inside me, the merits of all the good deeds done to benefit other people. Our parents taught us not to be greedy. Greed is the same whether it rules a rich man's heart or a pauper's, whether it consumes most shopkeepers, millers, members of parliament, senators, civil servants, generals, government officials, factory owners, hotel owners, bankers, business executives or thieves. Some of these wealthy and influential people have awesome power to log the forests, force millions of powerless beings off the land to build dams or to plant the harmful and fast growing eucalyptus trees in order to feed pulp and paper mills and exploit us to get rich fast. It is sheer greed that makes them do this. Like our father, I feel sorry for them. Because of greed, the greedy are never content. They always crave for more and much more, and so they do not have true happiness. I feel sorry for empty shop-houses that no one wants to rent or buy, and so being left to rust and rot. I feel sorry also for a luxurious hotel in our provincial town that has been closed by the bank, which in turn has been hard-hit by its own corruption. Do you know that one of the financial advisers of the bank has fled the country and is now fighting against extradition, that another financier from a failed financial firm also has taken flight to where you are now living?

It is heart-rending to see another huge hotel in our town left unfinished. What a sad state. What a waste, especially when two local schoolteachers, Tim Booning and Somjai Utrawichian, have been murdered for exposing corruption in our province. I feel sorry for so many unfinished buildings in Kroongtep, the Celestial City, exposing steel skeletons to the elements, rusting away. The photo we saw in the newspapers, which the headman brought from Muang, could say more than a thousand words. Just imagine the money and human energy that have gone to waste over them. What an eyesore! And these Monuments of Greed daily hit the eyes of the city people. These rusting gigantic frames of unfinished buildings may serve as the Monuments of Corruption as well for a long time to come.

Yes, I do feel very sad to read in the newspapers that there are more than two hundred unfinished construction sites and four hundred empty condominiums and offices that nobody will buy or rent. As you know, I am merely a poor and ignorant Esarn peasant who has no education further from Pathom 4, and certainly I am not an economist. Hence, I do not know what is happening to the economy. I wonder whether our bankers, financiers, entrepreneurs, property developers, politicians and the clever city dwellers know. Do you know? I wonder what kind of reaction some knowledgeable Thais had when they found out that many influential men, bankers included, were alleged to have siphoned off money from their banks, and financiers from their financial institutions. Some of them were said to have approved big loans without collateral or not even with faked collateral. The funds were then used to develop their private projects, property development schemes, hotels and shopping centres, apartment buildings, office buildings, restaurants, etc., while the banks were being sucked dry.

Then there are some greatly generous people who put enormous amounts of assets under the names of their household staff members including servants and drivers and guards. Is this because they want to enrich the poor souls who have been faithfully serving them? If it is so, they must be profiting hugely from their good deeds, their wonderful karma. Did you know that one such powerful and generous tycoon, who has been known to give one billion baht worth of assets to each of his seven servants, has become our very powerful leader? So it goes to prove that the good karma eventually boomerangs to reward the merit maker even in this life!

Meanwhile, more and more of our people have lost their jobs and returned to their home villages from the factories. I do not know exactly what this word 'laid-off' entails, but a lot of the so-called 'laid-off workers', who remain in the Celestial City, have been making demonstrations to ask for their last month's salaries, not to mention severance pay. I looked at the photos in the newspapers that reported the workers' protest with dismay. Now in our village the returned factory hands just hang around, having nothing to do. But they said the companies for which they worked gave them a hope that they would be given back their jobs when the 'rong-ngaans' could be reopened. Now the years have passed, and they are still hoping, waiting to be called back to their old jobs. Meanwhile, petty thieves prowl villages at night stealing whatever they can lay their hands on to survive. Even in daylight, we have to keep a close watch on our buffaloes. Some men from dog-eating ethnic groups, mostly from Sakol and Panom, come to look for dogs. Our Dum and Namtan and Spotty have been taken and we mourned their loss. These days you walk into quiet villages; there are not many dogs left to bark at you.

The reports that many politicians have been fighting tooth and nail for cabinet posts and top jobs in the money-making ministries continue to take most of the front-page space of the newspapers. It appears that they have the right to use the bought positions for their own advantage instead *of for the good of the country. It has been alleged that, having paid a high price for the appointments, there is a good reason that the rewards should be much higher than the amount spent on vote buying and bribery. One MP in our province was reportedly said to have spent 100 million baht to garner votes in an election. One of his vote canvassers was caught with 12 million in 100 baht bank notes stashed in his van a few days prior to the election date. So having invested so much money, it is considered that the buyers have the right to reap much more than the mere return of their initial investment, is it not?*

During the past years over five million people not far from us have been 'relocated' by force so as to leave the land to the concessionaires to plant eucalyptus trees in order to expand the pulp and paper industry. In certain areas, thousands have been moved out to give way to the construction of gigantic dams. The Moonmouth Dam is a case in point. This I know because it took place near us. This calamity-causing dam, built with a loan of 800 million US dollars from the World Bank, is said to be a flop. It has been reported that the damned dam could not generate electricity in the summer months due to insufficient flow of water. As a result it is left to rust and for taxpayers to pay the debt plus interest, despite immeasurable human suffering and the damage done to the people and the ecology. 'Ecology' is a new word for me. But I have begun to understand what it is when I read in the newspapers concerning the destruction of livelihood and the environment in the path of the construction of dams and the pollution created by the pulp and paper factories, sugar factories and flour factories in Esarn. Even now the severely affected people have to keep going to the Celestial City to ask for some compensation as well as attempting to stop the toxic waste from being discharged into the Pong and the Shee rivers.

Do let me know some basic truths concerning these issues. I do want to have some facts so that I will not feel that I have been lied to and go blindly through life. You, who have had more education than I, should be my reliable source of information so that I do not have to depend solely on the Thai dailies.

Meanwhile, in the face of change we are still at peace and content with our lot in life. As for me, I am prepared to be silent and would not lead our people to make a protest as long as we are still allowed to till our land, and not be brutally forced to move so as to give way for projects. I can hardly rise in revolt on my own for it is not my nature. Besides, most of our leaders have been killed, and recently an outspoken worker has disappeared without trace.

Shall I continue to listen to the wonderful promises the candidates made during election time? Have you ever wondered why a lot of the candidates tend to promise the world, using high-sounding words and jargon time and again? Would you believe that my vote was priced at 300 baht during the last election? No wonder only the very rich can become members of parliament and the overwhelmingly wealthy tycoons take top political appointments. I also read in the newspapers that there were eight MPs who were alleged to be involved in drug trafficking. I just cannot believe that some big men and important leaders in honourable and distinguished positions and high places could be involved in wicked activities. It is hard to believe that there were many godfathers, big time crooks, gambling den operators, brothel owners, paedophiles and extortionists among the senators and members of parliament, causing not only damage to their good and honest peers but also to the respectability of the institutions. If the newspapers had not printed their photos along with their names in the reports, I could not have believed these allegations. What have you read and heard? Do you still remember the Aesop's Fable we read when we were in Napo Primary School about a new batch of large blood-sucking gnats?

I want you to come back and run for a seat in parliament so that you can see and smell for yourself at close quarters. People like you should not stay away and let the very corrupt and extremely avaricious men run our country for their own gain. You have been away a long time now, brother. Another season is passing. Our rice is now being reaped. I am proud that these golden sheaves are the result of our hard work. The grain is life and gives the promise of plenty. One day you will return, I am sure. You will learn that there is no other place that can give you real happiness than your own home, among your own people. I remember so well our childhood. You, whom everyone called The Mute, used to be frail, feeble and vulnerable. I was afraid that you might not make it when you fell into the water or when you fell from the hut before that. Both times we had to put you on a bamboo rack over the charcoal embers. You recovered and grew up. No one could imagine that it would be the silent weakling who is now better off than any of us.

Father and Mother are getting old very fast now, but they still try to help as much as they can in the rice fields. I have to turn away when Mother gazes hopefully across the plain to where you might appear before her eyes.

We send you much love.

Kiang

The effort to finish the letter was quite a strain on Kiang, who had to grapple with high-sounding words and platitudes used almost daily by the media so that he could put it across to his learned brother in order to sound intelligent and philosophical. Having extinguished the kerosene lamp, he looked up at the stars, imagining the distance his letter would have to cover before reaching its destination. In his mind, Kiang tried to reach London but could not. He also attempted to be in his brother's place, should he be so bright and fortunate. Then he shuddered at the thought, fearing the departure from Napo, the life among strangers in foreign countries, and the difficulties in learning. So now he would be content only with being what he was, hopefully aiming to wed very soon.

Kiang began to be extremely serious about his marriage. But when he wanted to think, he found that his mind became vague and flitting. This frustrated him so much that he gave up reaping half-way through, and left the paddy with an excuse of going to shoot a bird or two to make a meal. He carried his bamboo blowpipe, striding across the plain towards the woods. Once he was far from all eyes, he discarded the pretense and sat under a tree, trying to think. But this extraordinary mental engagement aggravated him further for he could not concentrate or reach the heart of the matter. His mind drifted, recalling an image of Luke-pi as a tiny boy running against the rain, following the buffaloes, and as a poem reader being bullied by the chief of the buffalo-boy gang. Why must the Tadpole go away? Kiang wondered. What makes people go from place to place? The fretful man went further across the desolate plain, burdened with questions to which he could not find any answers. Aimlessly he moved on, hearing neither birdcalls nor the bellowing of buffaloes. He wanted to go away from Napo, from people, from himself. He missed his brother now, wanting to be told of life elsewhere, to know a little more. When he came to a stream shaded and cooled by a leafy tree he stood mindlessly, contemplating his reflection in the water. The distorted image told of leanness; it was all limbs and no flesh. Kiang wondered what he looked like to others. Taking off his baggy shorts to bathe, he thought of Teacher Kumjai due to the underwear, which had lost its original colour and become frayed. It took him back to the day the teacher had brought two pairs for him from the Heavenly City of Angels. The ones he had just taken off would not last for long now. When the elastic around the waist finally gave out, he would have to throw them away, and go back to the old days when he had done without.

This awareness saddened him for he knew there was no hope of having any others. But now, contemplating his nakedness, he felt his need for a woman who would bear his children. Then Kiang decided to elope with Poon Padthaisong, since he could not raise enough money for a dowry.

In London, there were moments when Prem Surin entertained a sense of joy. Looking back, he saw how his formative mind had been damaged during the sixteen years of the tyrannical Sarit Dhanarat's military rule, which the *Terrible Trio* inherited after the despot's demise in 1963.

Now he counted it as a blessing to experience freedom, a feeling that he had never felt before. It was both strange and exhilarating to be free, free to act, to speak, to be an individual and to be different. In London there was no one watching him, putting a limit on his reading, policing his maimed mind that was presently re-forming.

Often he went to Speakers' Corner in Hyde Park to listen to people from all walks of life calling attention to the accusations, grievances, ideologies and protests. The released Siamese compared himself to a fish that had left the stagnant murky water of an enclosed sunless tank for the cool, clear pool. He also entertained a sense of elation in his heart as he listened to each speaker whom he considered to be daring in challenging the authorities, expounding opinions and convictions in a forthright and aggressive manner. He wondered for how long had the British public enjoyed such rights and freedom, whether blood had been shed to win liberty and democracy as hundreds had to die in the streets of Kroongtep on the 14th of October 1973.

He recalled a phase in the history of Thailand when Prime Minister Plaek Pibulsongkram had toured Europe with his beloved wife Thanpuying La-iad and their entourage. While in London the party must have visited Speakers' Corner because on their return to Kroongtep, 'Poodhydepark' (Hyde Park Speech) was introduced to the Thai public, allowing aspiring speakers to use a corner of Sanarmluang to copy Speakers' Corner. Enthusiasm for it was so overwhelming that the thousands that gathered at the tamarind-lined ground could not find enough space to stand. But then Sanarmluang could hardly boast the same tolerance which Hyde Park enjoyed, for the authorities at the time did not share their British counterparts' attitudes. Moreover, it was unthinkable that there was graft, injustice, abuse of power, vote buying and suppression in Thai society. To speak openly of these matters in a public place was outrageous. It was indeed an extremely grave mistake to import theories and practices from abroad. How dare the people criticize and speak fearlessly about all that had been guardedly kept in the dark? Suddenly the Thai 'Hyde Park' became a place of mass arrests and was eventually banned.

How free and cheerful Prem felt now, believing that if he had died in the October 1973 massacre he would never have experienced joy and liberation. He was convinced that his effort to flee from the grip of the despots had been worthwhile.

His bed-sitting room in Elia Street, Islington, required that he should be self-sufficient. It was the first time in his life that he had to live on his own, fending for himself, living on his own resources, solving problems, facing himself in the narrow room he learned to call, after the fashion, *the bed-sit*.

The pleasures of being on one's own and the happiness from being liberated lingered on. Many a time the student sat, contemplating the growing collection of books on the shelves and on his desk. No matter how keen he could be, there would still be more and much more to read and more pleasure to be had from reading. Names flashed: Fielding, Richardson, Shelley, Johnson, Gibbon, Crabbe, Blake, Wordsworth, Coleridge, Byron, Shakespeare, De Quincey, Keats, Hazlitt, Sidney, Donne, Jonson, Pope, Burns, Spencer, Milton, for now the Autumn Term at the University College of the University of London had begun.

For a long while he sat, listening to his own thoughts: *Alone, absolutely alone here now, in a country where Kumjai might not have to disappear, where Rit Apaidham might have been spared.*

Tucked away from the main thoroughfare of City Road, Elia Street was reasonably quiet. His room was at street level, and he could hear footfalls or the rolling of beer bottles on the pavement when some drunks kicked them out of their way after the corner pub, The Duke, was closed for the night. *Yes, I might have been killed in the October 1973 massacre, Prem reflected. I owe my life to Pramae and Pra Sungwian. The latter prevented me from joining the demonstration with tens of thousands of students from various universities and colleges at Dhamasart University to show solidarity for the need of a constitution, the right to vote, for the abrogation of martial law and for freedom.*

In his life he had not known the true meaning of *freedom* or *democracy* until now.

Prem searched for words. He had often longed for their deliverance in a poetic form:

Otherwise it is a sacrifice,
living among foreigners –
a crow in peacock's feathers,
learning to read lips, with a tendency
to speak in parrot-like mimicry,
gaining new gait and new eyes...

What shall I do with these words spilled from my crippled mind? Prem pondered, looking at the sheet of paper upon which the ink had just dried. He heard the chuckles from those famous, cherished British poets!

November still had some bright and dry days. Taking a walk in a park or along the Thames was a change from the classes and being confined in the bed-sit and from reading. To feel the crisp wintry air, to witness daily the change of colours on leaves, was both comforting and stimulating. At the end of each day it was possible to confirm that he had survived the departure and stayed alive, and that the 'staying on' in England was enriching him, for now he had been avidly absorbing new experiences and impressions, and gaining new awareness from each day.

His first summer and autumn in London had passed, and he had been ill. Rains made the shortened days sombre, putting the need for winter clothes and an electric heater at the top of his want-list. Books still had priority, and hunting for more volumes at Dillon's in Torrington Place and at various bookshops in Charing Cross Road soothed away the pangs of being too long alone. In the streets one shivered with cold. London had seen too many homeless down-and-outs to spare sympathy. The teeming millions moved to and fro, filling and emptying the streets. He gawped at faces in Regent Street and saw landscapes of many countries, stared at paintings and sculptures in galleries and museums and perceived a beauty far beyond what his deprived mind could hold, making him yearn to be able to conceive and create a beauty of his own. He eyed merchandise in shop-windows and longed to possess some items that would give warmth and comfort so as to make the dreary bed-sit more cheerful. He wished for an encounter that might bring friend-ship or familiarity.

Shaftesbury Avenue led on to the throbbing heart of Soho. He moved along the small, dimly lit alleys, lured into sex-shops, accosted by painted faces. But it was not the prostitutes, the pornography and sex objects that he was looking for. It was just a bowl of noodles in a Chinese restaurant, where the peculiar smell and some Oriental features might bring home closer.

A waiter came to take his order. Prem's choice was fried rice with egg and prawns, taking care not to say *fly lice*. And he patiently waited for it.

Outside, the mist had enfolded all things, and with it came the drizzle. Where could one go after having appeased hunger with the monosodium glutamate-enhanced fried rice? Suddenly he dreaded an evening alone in his room, with only the company of dead poets and novelists. But it was no fun either to be lost in the streets of

Soho in the misty, freezing night with a chilling rain to give one a cold. So he hastened to leave the labyrinthine alleys.

"Hey, Chink!" one of the three muggers stopped him, pushing him against a wall, saying they had bet among themselves whether he was circumcised or not.

A knife flashed. First the plastic raincoat came off, then the jacket, followed by the shirt.

"Drop your pants!"

"You'd better do what he said, Chink," sneered the second thug with mock seriousness, playing on Prem's bare chest with the knife.

I am not a Chink, the frightened student wanted to say, but still he kept his mouth tightly shut, knowing it would be useless. Remembering that the Napo seer, Tatip Henkai, had asked him not to curse anyone, he obeyed.

The third hooligan stood apart, waiting for an easy mugging to be over. They could see he was just a lamb, a tiny prey on their way to bigger crime. In fact, it was more or less for fun and a little profit from his wallet, which did not contain much. Being pushed aside, the frightened little man fell over the trousers that bound his ankles. The comical, naked situation succeeded in giving pleasure to the audience of three. Then the ruffians moved off; one whistled and the others kicked his scattered clothes out of their way. The frightened student lay still on the pavement as if trying to count the grains of dirt where he had fallen. If there was a need to rise and go away, it was because there was another stranger looking upon his nakedness. The towering figure handed to the grounded monsoon man the shirt and the emptied wallet. The victim could see that the towering white man could not be another mugger or a sadist to inflict further injury. On the contrary, the polite *farang* in a cashmere overcoat turned away while the believer in the force of *karma* put on his clothes.

What can I say in a situation like this? The modern day Englishman may think it is ridiculous or childish if I tell him that it is retribution due to my bad karma from the previous life?

Accepting the raincoat from his rescuer, Prem was ready to move off. So it seemed that the two men would have gone their separate ways if the budding poet had not happened to go the way where the urbane *kon-ungrit* had parked his car.

"May I offer you a lift?" the graceful Londoner made an offer across his Rolls-Royce.

Despite the cultured voice of the well-bred and well-educated, the farang cannot reach me now, not when I have already withdrawn into a sanctuary in the soul of Etan, who had died on the Plain of Napo. In a flash, I have left far behind the interplay of brutality of the leather and jeans and the genuine gentility, between the cockney hooligans from the East End and the suave West End expensive-car owner.

"I've just come from a theatre not far from where we met. It was a tremendous performance of Oscar Wilde's *The Importance of Being Earnest*. Do you go to the theatre sometimes?" the driver asked, glancing towards his passenger.

You have neither inclination for theatres nor the need of other delights London has to offer.

"Operas, Concerts?"

You have only vague notions about these. Operas are beyond your reach and understanding. As for the concerts, you parted with many pounds just for an experience of a 'Prom' concert at the Albert Hall, but that was last August, and you have not been to any since. Yet you will never forget the joy of hearing for the first time Beethoven's Ninth and the looks of the conductor, Wilhelm Hagenbach.

"My name is Charles, Charles Tregonning."

What is in a name? You are still the Mute, Luke-gop, Luke-pi, the Buffalo Lover, the white-eyed Lao. Should you invite him in? It would be most out of place for a noble looking gentleman who speaks in such a cultured voice, wearing an immaculate suit!

Here in this cold, inhospitable room he had secretly attempted to create beauty of his own through verse and prose while the famous poets and novelists of the British Isles looked on. Now the room had never seemed so drab and bare. It exposed its needs to the substantial stature of the grandee of the old school who had gone grey at the temples, whose fair hair, kept slightly long and wavy, was neatly parted and combed towards the back of his head, where it became more curly. *Such must be the noble looks of the 'pudi-ungrit', the English aristocrats*, the buffalo boy harked back to what the clairvoyant had foreseen. *So destiny has brought my better to humble me, to make me feel inferior. In comparison to this over six foot tall and finely featured Englishman who sounds as if he had been to a famous public school, I am a little monkey, a twit. Otherwise, why should such a personage linger in a lower class part of Islington? His Rolls-Royce parked outside 21 Elia Street appears as out of place as its owner inside this one-bed, one-chair, one-man room.*

The gentleman's expensive gold watch and the gold signet ring on the little finger of the left hand spoke a sublime language of their own against the loud jabbering of an old narrow bed that was made up as a sofa in daytime. Moreover, the crude little chair bought from a second-hand shop in Upper Street squeaked. And when Charles Tregonning produced a gold cigarette case and a gold lighter, there was not a single ashtray in the place for him. The host remained standing, looking about at a loss, fiddling with the cup and the saucer.

"Will this do?" Prem asked and offered the saucer as an ashtray.

The guest was adjusting himself in the wooden chair, which protested rudely under the moving weight. Would an English gentleman ever dream of using a saucer as an ashtray in his castle? Charles Tregonning accepted the offer with a mild smile on his smooth, well-shaven face. Then the host could not offer a cup of tea. He had never anticipated that he would have to entertain any visitors. No, he would not offer tea. "Sorry, I haven't got around to buying another tea cup,' Prem lamely made an excuse.

Among thousands of things he had not learned was the mechanism of social grace and the art of conducting a conversation. Worse still, he had allowed a stranger to enter his private world, which he had kept alive with his longings and dreams, with the creativity that gave birth to poems and stories. So now it would be safer to talk of Thailand, its tourist attractions, answering questions with short or elusive remarks. Equally the suave, reserved Britisher promised no more than one could see from outside, should one be window-shopping for intimacy.

Brother! Why must you write in this vein? It is most disheartening and distracting to read your news, Prem Surin sighed after having read his brother's letter. *Don't you know that anxieties and insomnia are adamant adversaries to the studies? I need all the energy and concentration to cope with learning and writing. It is not only a pursuit of knowledge that is a goal but also the process of reasoning and thinking and opinion forming to rebuild a mind that has been stunted and crippled during the formative years by an age-old feudal educational system. I must go through the learning years in England, giving every minute to the task so that I would eventually emerge as a thinking person. You and I have been subjected to authoritative teaching and undergone rote learning, geared to bring about obedience, subservience and mindlessness. We are supposed to become unthinking, silent and submissive so as to be easily exploited and governable. You are not supposed to have an inquiring mind, asking too many questions and having critical thinking. You are not supposed to be opinionated, critical and forthright. You should never challenge or oppose the authorities in any way. Take care. Writing in such a vein could bring troubles to both of us. And should I respond to all your queries in detail and with candour, the answers would give me away too early in the game. Should they be intercepted or fall into wrong hands, I fear for our safety. Like a pregnant woman safeguarding the foetus in the womb, I have to take care of the seed in my head until it can be germinated and evolve into a full form. At present I have to keep the defiance and the effort to think profoundly and to write well hidden, so that in the meantime the deprived mind can be developed into a stronger and more capable thinking tool.*

Brother, it requires energy, time and a skillful means to secrete from my famished mind well-thought words to represent ideas and images conceived during the struggling years of our impoverished childhood. Once firmly embedded, the seed lay deeply dormant, waiting for the right time to grow. And I must nurture it to a proper height. This consuming force is driving me to deliver an end result, a book, on an agenda that belongs to fate rather than my own design.

Meanwhile, I pin my hopes on a learning process and on living in freedom abroad to salvage my deformed mind. I see myself as being one of the disabled trying lamely to keep abreast with those whose bodies and minds have been well nurtured and developed. Thus, I resort to using English as a crutch for support in order to attain some degree of order and discipline in reasoning and writing. Still, a great deal of childishness and gibberish utterances can come through. My tutor, Ian Hume, has now recognized that I, like many of our members of parliament and high-ranking government officials, have the mind of a twelve-year old English boy. As a result Hume is sympathetic and patient enough to guide me along a new path of learning and process of reasoning. At times it is discouraging to see that the way to salvation is a thousand miles away.

Though there is no armour to shield me from danger, I endure the fear. It is no laughing matter to put one's life on the line as ten murdered teachers in Esarn, our region, have done before. Yes, it is wonderful to be alive still.

I am always aware of it and appreciate every moment. It would be most pleasant and enjoyable to be at home with you and the herd, though my buffalo friend Etan has died, and her children Aitong and Edam have been sold. Could it be raining there at this moment? In London, the rain is horrible, but on the Plain of Napo, it means hope and joy. During or after the downpour, the frogs come out from hiding to croak and couple. The little boys and girls are happy too, catching the croaking creatures. There, in Esarn, most people are busy during the monsoon season. From dawn to dusk they are out in the open, ploughing the paddy fields and planting the rice.

It would be quite easy to do away with the scholarship and return home, but it would be miserable to live in the same way again – to be silent, absolutely unthinking and under suppression. Would it be a blessing in disguise to live poorly, in mute acceptance of one's fate and in all situations? Is it a mere idealistic dream to think that one could return home to live close to the soil, to marry a peasant girl and have children there in an Esarn village on the Korat Plateau far away from the traffic jams, pollution, falsehoods and corruption of the capital? Whether one would ever be happy there again is another matter. Admit it. You have been changed a great deal since the first departure. You have managed to escape. Now you are experiencing a different school, a different way of life. You know what it takes to be different at home. To be accepted is to be corrupted. Will you stand the test? You once bragged loudly that all you wanted was to help your country and its poor. It may sound a superfluous boast now, made in a distant time and place.

Yet the student had a hope. He trusted that there must be a way to salvage his maimed mind so as to become a creative person who might be able to help those who are less fortunate.

Mother and Son

This is Thailand

Seeing the bill-collector from the Electricity Authority, mother herded all of us into the darkest corner of the shanty.

"Keep quiet," she ordered.

Dust began to settle on us. I wondered how long she intended to conceal us.

"She must be in. I talked to her a moment ago," one of our neighbours told the bill-collector.

Mother raised her hands to her pallid face as if to hide it. How bony were her fingers; they could hardly cover her prominent cheekbones.

"Go. Tell him I've gone out. But don't accept anything from him," she whispered to me.

Being the oldest of her children, I had to face the official. Gingerly I left mother's protective arms and braved the situation.

"Nobody is home," I lied on mother's behalf and suffered no guilt for being a liar when one had to be untruthful to a heartless wraith of the authority.

The unheeding man continued to scribble words onto a piece of paper. Before I could do anything he shoved the note into my hand. Mother screamed when she saw what I handed to her later. "I told you not to except anything from him. Stupid boy! Idiotic you! Now I have to go to the district office to pay within seven days. If you hadn't accepted it, he'd have to come back next month. Now I'll have to raise money to pay the bill or else they'll come to cut the wires and take the meter away."

"Will they really, Mum?" I tried to sound most concerned.

"Of course, they will."

"How cruel. How they could be so heartless."

"What good have you done all day except making trouble eh?" she pulled hard at my ear. And after a few seconds of letting it go, she slapped my face.

Her collarbones became prominent as she heaved and sighed. By sighing and taking it out on me, her bad temper seemed slightly spent. True, these days I had stopped selling flowers and sometimes copies of the most popular newspaper at a congested intersection since the police had taken action to harass and arrest hawkers, including us street urchins who tried to make a pittance from selling whatever we could. But, as everyone knew, it had only been a blitz after a police chief had sent down orders, perhaps because someone wrote a letter of complaint to the newspapers. If we were in a position to pay regular protection money we would have been protected, and so allowed to continue our operation like drug trafficking, gambling, prostitution, sex shows and some other protected businesses. Soon the dust would settle and I could go back to the streets again. Meanwhile, I was to hide out in Bonkai Slum.

How could I guess, at the time, that mother was playing a waiting game with the bill collector? Within a month there might be money from father, who had gone to Singapore to work. He had been away from us for some time now. Mother took me with her to see him off at the airport. Did you ever see a taxi-driver in a suit? For once, in one's short life, to go abroad one must put on a suit, so he was told. Off to work on a construction site, to carry heavy objects, he looked more like a buffalo being taken to a slaughterhouse. Even for that kind of work, which the Singaporeans did not want to do, the employment agency fleeced him of all he had. Then they rounded up the *successful applicants* like a herd of wild cattle. Yes, most of these straggling workers looked wild but willing, coming from some forsaken Esarn plains.

At the airport check-in counters, they looked like a frightened pack of puppies huddling together while the group leader loudly told them that in Singapore they must not chew chewing gum, urinate in the lifts and in public areas, and for the smokers, they must try to give up smoking.

Before going inside the Departure Hall father came to ruffle my hair and said: "You little rascal, you behave from now on, okay? Don't stick your tongue out at policemen or they'd cut it off." He did not look at mother, I saw.

Meanwhile, mother continued to sell *kanomkok* on the pavement of Rama 4, not far from Lumpini Boxing Stadium and Bonkai Slum. She made it from rice flour, sugar, coconut milk and a few pinches of salt. Sometimes when she was in a good mood, some finely chopped spring onions would be added. Her customers were from all walks of life. The poor could make a meal out of her *kanomkok* for five baht, while the rich coming in their luxurious sedans satisfied their nostalgia for something down-to-earth and traditionally Thai. To the rich and poor alike, mother's voice sounded sweeter than we normally heard in our shanty.

Sometimes I stayed at her side and helped count the change. It was far better to be in touch with life, with the noise and the fumes from the congested traffic. I was tempted by the smell of food being, grilled, stir-fried and eaten on the pavement while the ululation was going on at high pitch, rather than being confined in the squalor of the hovel. I did not detest our home just because it was a rough shelter which father made from some old boards, discarded corrugated iron and softwood from unwanted crates shipped as containers from abroad. It was my love of the street life that kept me out most of the time, running about selling flowers and newspapers to motorists while they were stuck in the traffic at intersections. I wanted very much to be near the Rich Big Men and their Beautiful Women whose photos I saw, about whom I read in the newspaper that I sell daily, wondering whether they were the Ones. Though the steel car doors and thick glass windows, many of which were, I was told, bulletproofed, were between us, I could not help wanting to be close to angelic movie stars, famous television personalities, asset-hiding tycoons, be-suited business executives, pretty whores, respectable thieves and high-ranking crooks, opulently rich politicians, untouchable drug traffickers, renowned crime kingpins, invincible drug barons, awesome god-fathers, revered illegal casino operators, magnanimous vote-buyers, well-kept women, under-cover paedophiles, astute financial advisers who obviously had not yet fled the country, big loan approving bank presidents and their vice presidents, absolutely shrewd financiers some of whom might be on their way to the International Airport, wheeler-dealers of the stock exchange, manipulators, property developers in disguise so that creditors and bankers could not identify them, the silent tax payers and sex-struck foreign visitors with their cute partners. When you read everyday about these celebrities, knowing many of their names, seeing their faces in the newspaper that you sell, you do want to see them in the flesh when they are trapped in their vehicles in the traffic chaos. They could hardly go away from me, and I could get to be very near to them.

Yes, the traffic jams of Bangkok were notoriously mammoth. Millions of people sitting in their cars for many hours a day while their lives were ticking away towards death. Only I was free to roam at will. When some of these good people rolled down their windows to buy jasmine garlands from me, I'd hear the boom boom boom music from the car stereo, feel the cool air surging out to lick my sweaty face, and I could smell the distinctive scent of cured leather. At the closing hours of bars, nightclubs, and whorehouses, I'd see another kind of crowd: well-dressed pimps and their pretty cash earners on motorcycles, staggering drunkards, jolly gays coming out of their bars and saunas, male and female prostitutes, sexy a-go-go dancers and scantily dressed pole dancers, adulterers on their way to or from short-time motels, bartenders going home and taxi drivers in their cars waiting for customers. My own father, when he was still a taxi driver, did that too, parking his run-down Toyota close to popular haunts which helped make Bangkok renowned as the whorehouse of the world, attracting millions of visitors from so many countries. Being a taxi driver Father must have seen daily these fascinating people. And I could not help being attracted to them, wanting to be a part of their interesting lives. I believed that some of them had sympathy for me too, seeing me staying up as late as they were. Kind with advice, once one of them said to me: "A little boy like you should be in bed now. Go home." But advice was useless to me. No matter how late it was, all I wanted was to make more money so the last baht would bring my total earning for the day and night to a twenty baht bank note which I would put in mother's hand on showing my face at home. So the pseudo paternal tone of voice urging me to go home at two in the morning did not work. I stayed on in the streets though the whole world seemed to have given up their roles for the night. Pimps ceased to be pimping; bar girls took off their false eye-lashes and jumped on the backs of motorcycles, while bar tenders changed their uniforms for street clothes; and prostitutes gave back their number badges to the brothel operators. Only I maintained my role of a street vendor to the end.

Once, among the chaos, my own father eased his rusty Toyota towards me. He had a passenger with him, and he said loudly: "Look at that little daredevil. Let's run him down." And he nearly hit me, snatching a copy of Thai Rath from me. I demanded payment though he was my father. As a result he slapped me and then rolled up his window, and moved off when the traffic light turned green. Sometimes, when he was resting with us at home, he told us: "It's a shame. You boys create a bad image for the country. What will the tourists think of us?" Father did not laugh. "Now, Tui, you rascal. What will you say to that?"

"Why, Dad, you can bring tourists to see us in this slum."

For they might see something closer to the truth.

I wanted so badly to hang on to my job because to be allowed by the Master of the Territory to make a living and to guard my own turf was not easy. Besides, the Master of the Territory must be pleased with what you could give him daily. Otherwise, you would not be able to show your face there. Father understood me well since he was in the same boat, having to rent the crummy car from a taxi operator on a daily basis.

Like selling one's body to give pleasure to others or one's soul to the devil, selling flowers and newspapers at jammed intersections had its stress and strain. Many other kids had to resort to inhaling thinner to keep them going. Not I. I could be alert and awake in the wee hours so I would not miss an opportunity, not so much in selling but in seeing some of the dignitaries and celebrities mentioned earlier. And having seen a lot of them after a while, I could laugh. It was amusing to see that while we, unprotected street boys and girls, were being harassed and arrested and condemned, murderers, drug traffickers, drug pushers, the bribers and the bribed, corrupt officials, the swindlers, the disguised property developers (whose buildings were left empty or unfinished exposing steel rods to the elements, rusting away), bankers who caused their banks to crash, financiers who embezzled billions, gunmen for hire, whores and pimps were riding by as free as could be. I wonder why the police never pick their own size or bigger, while we tiny little boys and girls who struggle to survive have to suffer a rather unfair treatment. Well, *maipenrai*. Never mind. This is Thailand. I could patiently wait and stay by mother, helping her count the change.

At home, one day, mother said to me: "Don't sneak off anywhere now. You look after your brothers and sisters. I'm going out to gamble."

Then she went off hopefully. But as soon as she left the shack for the gambling den belonging to a senator, I left too. Breathlessly I reached the street and felt a great relief to be out of the squalid slum. I loitered at the spot where mother normally sold *kanomkok*, to watch trucks, cars, taxi, tuk-tuks, motorcycles, passers-by, and to be a part of life on Rama 4. Suddenly a car halted in front of me, and two well-dressed ladies came out. Daintily they looked about. Seeing me, they asked: "Where is the *kanomkok* woman today?"

"She's gone to gamble at a senator's illegal casino," promptly said I.

Mother's customers looked disappointed. One said to the other: "Ah, she exercises her freedom! And you talk of the poor wanting to become Communists."

I did not understand what she meant, but then they moved off, back to the waiting Benz. Soon hunger gnawed, so I went back to the hovel to take my share of whatever was left in an aluminium pot. The small ones were all crying because one of them had fallen into the slime, which was as old and stinking as the city itself. I washed the black mud off his face just in time. Mother came back sooner than expected; from her expression, I could tell that she had lost at the table, enriching the senator a little more. Poor mum, she did not say much while fumbling among boxes in a corner not dark enough to conceal her sadness and despair. She was fondling a small gold ring.

"Put it on, Mum," urged I.

She did, but the ring could not stay on any of her fingers.

"I've worked myself to the bone," she moaned, having that far away look in her eyes.

Whether she was going to pawn it afterward, I could not tell. But after having seen how she caressed the ring, I went out immediately to brave the police. I did not care what I would or could do to bring in some money.

The seven days of grace the bill collector gave us had passed, but we were relying on the usual inefficiency of bureaucracy, hoping that the electrical wires would not be cut and the meter taken away so promptly. Each day meant a lot to Mother.

"Why hasn't your father sent any news and money?" she asked wearily again and again.

"Maybe he has already," said I to console her, "but then it could be delayed or lost along the way."

We hoped in vain. The men arrived, cut the wires and took the meter away. It was staggering to know now that the Authority could be punctual, concerning its own benefits.

"Go and see whether you can ask a shopkeeper to sell you a few candles on credit," mother hoped. "Don't go to the shop in front of the lane where they know you. Go farther."

Even though we had lived in poverty all our lives, she still cared very much about losing face. For having to resort to candles would tell tales.

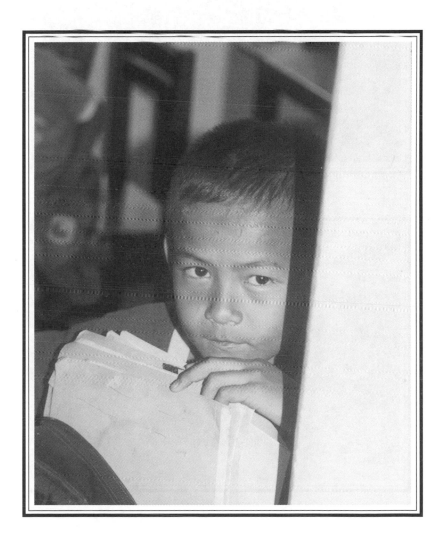

The Force of Karma

The war to win the people

Deep in the heart of Esarn, the outlaws made their attack at Fungshu Creek, where the track dipped into a shallow stream. Deep in the mud, the jeep revved vehemently. At that moment, guns were fired from both banks. The driver and his two passengers had only a second to scream. Their bullet-ridden bodies slumped languidly, covered by the shattered windscreen. Coming out from the bushes, the killers took their time to relish their triumph, for this remote territory was one of their strongholds.

Following that victory, the outlaws preyed on prominent middlemen, tyrannical thieves and rapacious usurers who sought protection from the police instead of lessening their greed and strong-arm tactics. Some of these unyielding grabbers went further to urge an insurgent suppression regiment stationed near Muang to take full control of the region, claiming that the attacks were assaults from the Communists. The military reacted swiftly when the headman of Napo and three of his henchmen were brutally butchered.

The presence of the force in the district promised a sense of security but then after the American-trained and equipped contingent had moved elsewhere the onslaught resumed. Police stations and military outposts were among the casualties. At night, fearful inhabitants huddled within their huts. Only at daybreak did they dare to come out into the open.

Early in the morning Prem Surin, the Pundit Piksu, one of the two monks residing at Wat Napo, went out for alms along the village lanes. He sensed the emptiness, a void made by the absence of most men. Napo had become a village of the aged and the very young when able men and women had gone away to factories and plantations in far off places. Many persons had disappeared without trace. Sounds of shouting and joyful laughter were rare.

Yet a number of old women still continued to offer him food.

The warmth of the steamed rice in the begging bowl seemed to reassure the priest that the spirit of Napo remained. While emptying the contents upon returning to the temple after the alms receiving round, he discovered that a little piece of paper was attached to a boiled egg. Having carefully detached it, the *piksu* read: *Kroo Kumjai is still alive.*

Toon Tinthaisong (formerly 'Puthaisong') had put into his begging bowl the boiled egg that morning. At first he could hardly believe the message, but later he welcomed it as a source of hope. At an appropriate time he would inquire after Kumjai Chaiwankul, the former teacher of the ruined Napo Primary School. At that instant a mental image of Lord Buddha held him in check. The priest reminded himself that he should not be moved by emotions, words and deeds. Therefore, the elation brought about by the tiny piece of paper that bore Toon's handwriting must be suppressed. The young monk must not allow the old abbot and several grey-headed men and women and the recently elected headman, congregating in the hall, to detect the hope and joy that were blossoming on his face.

After the monks had finished their breakfast, Singhon Homhaul, the new headman, cleared his throat and raised his voice so that the priests and the lay people in the *sala* would hear him.

"Since my first month as the *khamnan* (headman), I've been trying to bring electricity to Napo. Now we will have it in less than three months," Khamnan Singhon paused to observe how the venerable abbot would react to the news, expecting at the same time to receive praise from the audience for his progressive drive. But the trembling holy man could only manage to say one word, which sounded more like a grunt than 'good'.

"Without electricity, we cannot have television, electric rice cookers, refrigerators, electric fans and washing machines," said the headman louder.

A seventy-year old peasant who managed to catch some of the headman's words wanted to ask what electric rice cookers and refrigerators and washing machines were, but he dared not. Several Napotians had seen a television set when they went to Muang to sell their rice. The mill owner had it on loudly the day another revolution took place to replace a civilian government with military dictatorship.

"And I've also the other good news," Singhon emphasized the last two words. "We're going to have an all-weather road to link Napo with Muang." Having said that, he smiled broadly. Certainly the two major development projects under his authority would boost his power base, but when there was no sound of delight or applause from the gathering he turned to the abbot, who was rinsing his mouth.

Glancing at the submissive, mild-mannered men and meek women, Pundit Piksu recalled Kroo Kumjai's dictum heard under the thinly thatched shack called Napo Primary School: *Changes are inevitable; they can be sudden and brutal at one time or they can steal upon us like thieves in the night at another. I want to prepare you to face the changes in your lives.*

Yes, changes are unavoidable, silently confirmed Prem, the priest, who could recall Lord Buddha's teaching on the subject: *All is transient; nothing is permanent.*

Trying to muster the attention of monks and men, Khamnan Singhon resorted to speaking in Siamese, the language of the Masters, instead of their Lao, in addressing the lower order, the peasants: "Lately, I've despatched thirty men from our district to work in the Middle East. Soon they'll come back with a great deal of money. Yes, their pockets will be full of cash when they return. They'll want to have television sets, electric rice cookers, refrigerators, sound equipment, electric fans and a good road, not just a rough track that makes Napo inaccessible in the rainy season. Some of them will be rich enough to buy vehicles. They won't think of becoming Communists then."

Since mute acceptance had become the norm, the audience wordlessly accepted the announcement and later quietly departed, leaving the headman to confer on some other matters with Luangpor Boon, the aged abbot, and Pra Prem, the young monk. Despite his great age and the priestly life, Luangpor Boon had not completely ignored worldly affairs. Money had always been so irresistible a temptation that the so-called *budgets,* public funds, grants and foreign aid became a lure. At the mere mention of big words like 'World Bank loans', 'accelerated development projects', 'regional irrigation schemes', 'dam constructions', 'the Green Esarn Campaign' or even the mundane sounds of 'road construction and maintenance' Luangpor Boon's heart withered with a knowledge of the extent of bribery, kick-back taking, cheating and the exploitation involved.

He knew that the previous headman and his cohorts had done extremely well for themselves when an era of 'intensive development projects' dawned on the district. Not being satisfied with creaming off the funds and taking bribes and the commission from the purchase of materials at an inflated price, they had cleverly devised two *projects* (a word often used by government officials) called the *Agro-*

Aid to Farmers and the Greening of Esarn to enlist members. Under the schemes, Montree Deesakul, Sanan Rakchat and Kriangkrai Chavalitpakdipol (formerly Peng Pakpoom), the three henchmen, had gone about, collecting membership fees, and then selling fertiliser of inferior quality or in some cases fake stuff to the farmers at an exorbitant price.

To help him swindle and take as much as possible out of his tenure, the *khamnan* had trained the three wraiths in the art of rapacity. These were his exact words at the beginning of the training: *In whatever you do, be sure there is a perfect fit, no loose ends, that all is clear. Have them come to meet you and write the numbers on paper, then tear it up and throw it away. Don't go and say: For this ten thousand, for that twenty thousand, and for those thirty thousand...*

Using Kriangkrai as a front, an agency had been set up to send labourers from Napo and other villages to work overseas. The *khamnan* could have seen that the business was a gold mine when each aspiring worker had to pay a fee of 100,000 baht up front even before they could obtain their passports. This was so huge a sum that most of the job seekers, using land title deeds as collateral, had to borrow money from loan sharks at five per cent per month. Then after half a year had gone by, the headman had claimed that the agency in the Celestial City took the money and did not produce the passports, the air tickets and the jobs for the applicants. Kiang Surin and Tongdum Tinthaisong, Toon's husband, were among the cheated men who had lost not only their entire farmland and the plots on which their houses were built, but also their livelihood. As a result, the destitute men disappeared one night to join Kumjai Chaiwankul and the band of *K-Force* fighters in Srisurachwood. A few months later, when the insurgents had attacked the headman's house, it was Tongdum's cry that was heard on top of the gunfire: 'He's for me! The *khamnan's* head is for me!' so that Kiang stepped aside to give the crier the chance to pierce the wicked man's heart several times, crying: "For Grandfather Sa. My knife for their bullets!" before the head would be severed.

"I hope you haven't forgotten why and how your predecessor and the three *luke-nongs* (minions) were murdered," said the wise abbot to the successor.

But Singhon Homhaul had not yet become expertly experienced in the art of cheating, graft and grabbing. Glancing sideways, he said, to assure the holy man:

"I knew who did it and who were their sympathisers. I've given all their names to the Insurgency Suppression Unit."

Despite his fifty years in the priesthood, the quivering abbot was still capable of sarcasm: "How clever of you. Have you anything else to say to me?"

"Oh yes, your venerable. A military propaganda unit has arrived and will hold an exhibition and a film show this evening. Perhaps the temple ground would suit the purpose, if you'd give permission."

"I don't like any kind of propaganda or entertainment here, but if I say no to you, you'll hold it against me and put my name down in your black book as being anti-government or a Communist sympathiser. I'll have to say yes, won't I?"

The steaming cup of tea soothed the ancient disciple of Lord Buddha. After the man had gone away, he breathed more easily though the hand lifting the cup trembled noticeably. Soon, he would have to cope with the blasting sound from the loudspeakers from the rally when the war to win the people began.

Peace did not last long, for now on the temple ground a group of men in fatigues and armed with war weapons started to erect a movie screen and rows of large display boards. Meanwhile a four-wheel drive was creeping along the village lanes, turning on at full blast its public address system to tell the wary dwellers of the coming event.

"Highly respected fathers and mothers, most beloved uncles and aunts, dearest brethren, we are pleased to have an opportunity to come to Napo. We hope all of you will show your support and your love for the nation by attending the exhibition and the movie show at seven o'clock this evening at the temple. Seven o'clock this evening, at the temple, all together, most revered and beloved brethren."

A patriotic song punctuated the announcement at regular intervals.

A group of squatting Napotians under a tamarind tree followed the vehicle with their eyes as it passed them, and after the ear-splitting volume was lessened by the distance, one of them said: "Isn't it nice to be their *most respected and beloved brethren*. When I was in the Celestial City last summer, one of the celestial people shouted at me as I was trying to cross a street at a pedestrian crossing. Mind you, I was careful, but all of a sudden I heard a frightful screeching sound so close to me. A car nearly hit me. It stopped only a few inches from me and scared the hell out of me. Before I could move, the driver pulled down a window and shouted *'you stupid Lao'* at me, when I was a labourer at a rice silo."

"Of course you're Lao, and stupid to boot to work as a coolie all day for a pittance," the one who was given a name of *Cretin* said.

"They called me *keeka* (shitty slave)," contributed a young man who had worked in an animal feed factory.

"Now it's fantastic to become their most revered and dearest, isn't it? I hope to hear this more often. If I had been their most beloved when I was a slave in a soft toy factory a few years ago, I'd never have left the place," piped one of the women. She did not know how lucky she was to be still alive today, when 188 of her colleagues had been burnt to death and 400 other workers injured during the fire that razed the factory to the ground a day after her departure.

The group ceased conversing when the same jeep returned, blasting them again, but this time with the national anthem. Hence, they rose, for they had been ordered by the headman to do so every time they heard it. In total obedience, they stood ramrod while the anthem lasted.

At the temple, adults and children alike crowded around the display boards, looking at propaganda materials being exhibited. These were posters depicting the atrocities of the Communist take-over in Cambodia. They were more or less the same display seen time and again every time the propaganda unit came to Napo. But then one could always gawk in awe at the pictures of the fleeing refugees, of the piles of skulls and bones, at the images of the destruction of houses and horrible death, at the description of the landlords, merchants, middlemen, and money lenders being publicly shot. At seven o'clock onward, the speeches on the importance of unity and love for the country commenced.

In his narrow room, Pra Prem endured the nerve-rending explosive sounds that were piercing his mind with messages of the conflicts between the rich and the poor, the masters and the oppressed, the exploiters and the exploited, and of the left and the right. Unlike the stoic abbot, the young priest was not aware of all the changes that had taken place in the region and in his own family.

Due to the disappearance of his brother Kiang and the loss of the farmland as well as the land on which Kiang's house stood, Poon, his sister-in-law, and her children had sought shelter under the Surins' roof. No one wished to talk of these happenings for fear that the monk would be disturbed. They thought it best that Pra Prem should remain a monk for several years. Simple and ignorant as they were, they believed that he would be safe, clothed in the yellow robe, residing in Wat Napo.

Also, Prem did not know that there were only Piang Charoenpol and Poon Surin to reap their rice while Grandfather Kum, the patriarch, had been bedridden with a recurring illness. His wife, Grandmother Boonliang, who had become bent and wizened, found herself with an increased number of grandchildren. But she accepted the predicament with her great capacity to endure. Without complaint, she took care of the sick and the young, with love and tenderness.

Bae Charoenpol, Piang's husband, had been sent as a labourer to Saudi Arabia so that he would return in two or three years with his pockets full of money as Khamnan Singhon had proclaimed.

Meanwhile, Pundit Piksu was thinking of leaving the priesthood. He wished to return to the world of men and dutifully take care of his parents, his nephews and nieces so that the boys and the girls would have proper food and go to the school that he determined to rebuild now that the previous headman had been killed. But then he was concerned with the question of how the abbot could keep the *Wat* going on his own without a younger monk to help him. Would there be one or two more men to be ordained soon? Most young and able-bodied men had gone away from Napo, to cities and abroad. Several had joined Kumjai Chaiwankul and the *K-Force* of brigands.

In the midst of his thoughts, Luke-naam, the temple boy, came into the room and kneeled.

"The *farang* who came with the soldiers wants to see you, Venerable Brother," chirped the cheeky acolyte.

The monk sat silently still as if he did not hear while the *luke-sith* retreated to the door. A moment later the visitor knocked and entered. Despite his sturdy frame, the brown-haired, hazel-eyed American did not seem awkward to sit cross-legged on the wooden floor. The *adviser,* who had just turned forty whilst on the road with the propaganda unit, wore a dark blue short-sleeved shirt and black trousers. His crew cut made him look younger than his age. Big-boned and rugged, the CIA agent reminded the priest of a German policeman who escorted him to the Narcotics Squad in Munich on the 23rd of December 1975. Pra Prem's heart suffered a quick, sharp pang, while the images of Helmut von Regnitz and Wilhelm Hagenbach loomed. Why must a reminder of European high culture, honour and probity recur at such an awkward moment? He had already shorn his head and put on a yellow robe to turn his back on the world of procreation and artistic creativity. He had got rid of his European clothes, had destroyed the concept of time and all the unpublished poems written in English, his handiwork hewn out of an attempt to overcome the maimed mind and the pain from the conflict of the East and the West. He believed that in an insignificant monastery of a forgotten hamlet of the impoverished Burirum Province in Esarn he could be beyond reach.

"I was told that you've been to Europe," Lucern Schultz, the third generation American was saying.

"I went as a student but returned as a drop-out because the studies in England were not based on rote learning as in Siam. I failed miserably. I became a hippy," the ordained one softly said, surprised that he could still be earthly convivial and in English, which he had not used for so long.

"You certainly have a *posh* accent," the Virginian complimented.

"That's from being forced daily by my flatmate, an Anglophile Siamese from one of the wealthiest and most powerful families, to speak with a stiff upper lip and listen to the debates in the House of Lords and to the recordings of Sir Charles Cuthry's aristocratic voice. Sir Charles is an Etonian, you know." *And Danny von Regnitz-Pilakol daily put a pressure on me to mimic the accent of the English upper classes. He ordered me to go to The Berkeley to sit and drink at The Blue Bar and I must talk with a fellow drinker who happened to be there next to me. He reasoned that I'd learn to overcome my timidity in face of the grandeur and elegance and so gain confidence and poise as well as putting into practice my newly acquired plummy accent. That was where I met for the first time Lord Bewley of Knightsbridge. Of course, the tryst was pre-arranged without my knowledge. I must admit that the aristocrat acted so well his part in the conspiracy. Yes, it was a nasty trick that Danny schemed to set him on me, a sacrificial lamb. And there, in the opulent hotel, the Lord instantly took the peasantry out of me as I stuttered and stammered and could not switch on the upper class accent and air. It was indeed one of Danny's nastiest tricks to make me walk into the trap. But all the same I continued learning and practising the accent so that I would not shame him in front of his aristocratic friends with the tongue of the lower classes, especially that of the East Enders, the Cockneys. And I obeyed him. To what end, I had no idea at the time, but only to be silent, fearful and in hiding in the sanctuary of the monastery now.*

Their conversation moved pleasantly on. The man from Langley, Virginia, had obviously become accustomed to Siamese ways, adopting the sitting posture of an obsequious Siamese, seemingly pleased to find in a troublesome spot in Esarn a monk with whom he could speak with the fluency of his own tongue. Pundit Piksu resumed a well-composed grace and reminded himself not to argue in the manner of laymen, when the subject of insurgency was raised:

"Twelve per cent of the villagers in these parts have become hard-core Communists and sixty per cent their sympathisers."

The monk did not appear alarmed. He replied calmly: "To me, they're people, my people. I know most of them well."

Had the CIA gathered the information that Kiang Surin was his brother?

"Communists are much against religions," Schultz hammered. "You won't remain a monk a day longer under Communism."

"It won't come to that," Pundit Piksu sounded confident. "A handful of peasants, using armed struggle tactics, cannot defeat the mighty Siamese military forces and those of yours. I speak of what I know locally, of course."

"With respect, Honourable Brother, you should open your eyes to the world beyond your district. Look at what happened in Vietnam, Cambodia and Lao. They're not so far from you."

"I know. I'm not blind. But obviously we could barely behave like the Vietnamese. Here, the straggling bands of outlaws and the survivors of the October 6th 1976 massacre don't stand to win. However, they fight on *for vengeance is theirs.* And also they don't want the powerful swindlers, the eminent crooks, the punitive murderers, the blatant thieves, the exceedingly corrupt politicians and bureaucrats, and the terrible tyrants to get away with their exploits, murders, stealing, vote buying, asset-hiding, money laundering and drug trafficking all the time. As for you, it's clear that you haven't learned anything from the defeat in the Vietnam War and from supporting the dictators, the tyrants and the most corrupt. You go on supporting them as long as they claim to withstand socialism and uphold capitalism regardless of how corrupt and tyrannical they can be. You were defeated in Vietnam in spite of the loss of thousands of American lives and the death of millions of Vietnamese, Cambodians and the Laotians, at the cost of billions of dollars. And yet it seems you haven't learned a lesson and become wiser. Even today innumerable civilians in these ravaged countries are still being killed or maimed by land mines, and continue to suffer as a result of the blanket bombings, the napalm bombs and the so-called 'agent orange', the defoliant chemicals that destroyed the woods, poisoned their water for generations to come. You seem to have convinced yourself, the world's police force, the defender of capitalism, that the bombings and the killings were just and worthwhile as long as they are being waged in other countries, presently in the Middle East. I don't have to be a reputable seer to see that more wars will be waged on new grounds and against new enemies. The bombings and killings will not end since when one 'terrorist' is killed ten more take his place, and so on. The atrocities created by *all* sides will not dissipate into thin air. They will bounce back at *all* perpetrators. It's the force of *karma*, my good man. But for you, the talk of *karma* may sound superstitious and ridiculous. As a Christian you may take to a saying of *As a man sows, so shall he reap*. It's the same thing. I may live to regret saying this but you've sowed a hell of a lot of missiles and bombs over many lands, unheeding that the force of *karma* or what we sow will catch up with all of us even within our lifetime. Some non-Buddhist fanatics or, I dare say Islamic extremists, may not take your wrath and 'retaliation' lying down as most good Buddhists may do. The more the warriors sow missiles and bombs and spray the bullets, the faster they bring Nostradamus' predictions to reality. And when they do, your president would proclaim 'anger' that would lead to 'retaliation' or perhaps he would opt unwisely to use the word 'crusade' instead of 'sorrow' that might bring about some wisdom. For now, as I speak, I fear for you and your adversaries who do not believe in the wisdom of non-violence and tolerance. The retaliations from both sides become more atrocious than before while we blame the other as the perpetrator, being blind to our own actions and reactions, considering the fight as a must or a just cause.

Now, at this very moment, I can hear a voice in my head warning me to speak compassionately or not at all. For being concerned with your safety and the lives of millions of innocent bystanders, Americans as well as their 'enemies' who shall suffer abominably though they have no part in the atrocities, I must speak. Are you aware of what Nostradamus foresaw?"

Despite his effort to sound compassionate, the age-old sentiment, which had lain deep in the heart, had thus emerged. The practising disciple of the Lord Buddha could see, in his mind's eye, the rearing ghastly head that should have been quashed in the earliest phase of priesthood so as to make the ordination pure and holy. Hence, he must lose no time in subsiding it. *I've failed as a compassionate follower of the Enlightened One*, Pra Prem realized. *I have failed utterly, my Lord.*

"Nostrada who? I've never heard of him. In this day and age, you shouldn't believe in silly seers or grasping fortune-tellers, dead or alive. Your venerable doesn't have to be afraid. We Americans are so great and powerful that there is no one who can make a tiny dent in our pride. But would your people, who claim to be Buddhists, cease to commit further atrocities or bad *karma* and be compassionate enough to lay down their arms to be pardoned and so come back to society even though they have not accomplished their vengeance? You may not know that the military has announced an amnesty campaign. If the insurgents surrender and lay down their weapons, they'll be pardoned. They can return to their homes," Lucern Schultz said unflinchingly.

"Unconditionally?"

"There are some conditions, of course. For example, they must not be politically active for the rest of their lives."

At that point one of the armed military personnel with a walkie-talkie came to ask the American to return to his jeep for now the propaganda unit would depart. After the team of awesome visitors had gone, Pra Prem prepared to lie down, spreading the rush mat on the floor and setting up his mosquito net. As he was about to extinguish the lamp, a piece of paper was tossed through the window. He quickly got hold of it and then went to close the door before reading:

Venerable Brother,

I have much to tell you, but hardly know where to begin. The last time we saw each other was when I went to Wat Borombopit before I took to Srisurachwood, and that was nearly eight years ago. Please forgive me for not having properly explained my action. I entered the forest to save my life, but then I got involved with a Chinese splinter group of bandits, the Chin Haw, who had escaped from the battle at Kaoko in Petchaboon. After the October 6th 1976 massacre of thousands of students in Dhamasart University and in the streets of Kroongtep, a number of survivors joined us. As we moved around the countryside, there have been frequent clashes with the police force and insurgent suppression units, but we have advantage over our enemies due to our knowledge of the terrain and we could often inflict heavy casualties on the government forces. Often, we run out of food supplies. Once we fell into a trap in a Nadhone village where we went in to collect food and medicine. During the fighting, one of our men fell next to me, and I quickly put my ID card in the dead man's pocket so that those who wished me dead would be satisfied. Only later I realized the effect the news had on our people. For one, the Venerable Brother Sungwian Suwanapumi, whom you served in Wat Borombopit, disrobed and came to join us. He is with us still, despite the fact that I am still alive. You might not know that he and I were born in the same village and became 'siaw', bonded with a vow of brotherhood.

It is best for you that I should not discuss here the ideologies and my cause so that you are free to choose your own kind of struggle. But whatever you want to do, don't do it now. Stay safe in the Wat as a monk. Please believe me and do as I ask, at any cost, until it is safe for you to leave the sanctuary.

My friend Sungwian took this course because we are bonded by the vow of fellowship. You and I have a bond too, but with your intelligence, you'll know what to do. There are many kinds of struggle. As for me I have no choice except to choose the armed struggle. Your brother, Kiang, and Toon's husband, Tongdum, and several Napotians including Panya Palaraksa, the village's versatile musician, joined us out of sheer necessity to survive as free men. Kiang and Tongdum have their bitterness and hatred. I don't know about Panya. Do you remember Panya? You took first and he came second then Toon third in your final year at Napo Primary. It still amazes me how musical he is. He can put a leaf between his lips and make a delightful sound to soothe us in the depths of Srisurachwood when we feel so weary.

I believe that destiny does not want you and me to meet again as yet. One day soon, we will see each other, I am sure. I have intentionally kept your name and our relationship out of every liaison so that you shall not be linked and get involved and punished. I want you to know this. Please do not react impulsively to this letter out of gratitude, for your action will bring danger not only to yourself but also to your family members who are still in the village. You're not in England, where you may walk freely no matter what your political beliefs, ideologies and preferences are.

Once, when we stopped in a place after a trek through the forest, I told Kiang, Tongdum and Panya what I truly believe in, and I am pleased to say that they have changed a great deal from when they first set out to accomplish their revenge. Panya seems the most relaxed and less serious among us. He is the only one who can occasionally laugh. If he had been allowed, he would have made a flute from bamboo and enchanted the woods with music.

Destroy this letter as soon as you have read it, so that it will not cause any harm to yourself and to others. I long for the day I can walk into Napo and teach again.

With most respectful regards,
Kumjai

2

Having extinguished the lamp, the monk went inside the mosquito net and laid down on his back. *How far could the mysterious messenger have gone by now?* Prem the priest pondered. I'll do what Kumjai has asked me to do. In his mind, he followed the footsteps of the cunning courier, who must be heading back to the woods where Kumjai, Kiang, Tongdum, Panya and the rest of the outlaws were lying low, protected by leafy boughs and bracken. Pundit Piksu imagined that he could hear the cicadas and the crickets and the hoots of owls and the cries of wild animals. But then he was suddenly reminded of the CIA agent whom he had entertained in this very room. Troubled by his own words spoken in the heat of the moment, the monk turned to lie flat on one side with his eyes open to the darkness. How strange it was to have a foreign visitor from another continent in this austere cell so far away from New York and Washington D.C. Until then he had not opened his heart to anyone since his departure from London. He had not talked openly to anybody about anything. And then, all of a sudden, he had abandoned the precaution and carelessly opened his heart to a spy!

Now, a long hand of the West had reached him, pointing out to him his need to communicate. But then how far away the world of Elizabeth Durham and Dani Pilakol, the world of the intellect, the world of Lord Bewley, Lord Norbury and Charles Tregonning, the world of nobility, art, fashion, gourmet dining and sophistication, the world of Wilhelm Hagenbach, the musical world of Europe, seemed to be. In England and Germany he had come to experience the delights of sensual pleasure, the freedom of an individual, the pain of conflicting cultures, and the knowledge that a bottle of a certain wine could cost fifty years of the Surins' hard labour to grow rice and turn the crop into cash at 280 baht a year. *Wilhelm ordered a bottle of that wine as if he had frequently done so, without a thought of the exorbitant price it commanded, while I trembled inwardly for the memory of a meal in Napo that was prepared from a small fish pounded into paste with chilli, shallots and salt to give flavour to boiled vegetables for the whole family.*

Now the fretful priest felt a sharp pang in the heart, thinking of the orchestral conductor, for it had not been a happy affair, unlike his involvement with Elizabeth Durham. As classmates at University

College, she and he were in their early twenties, viscerally driven by unbridled sexuality, which was fashionable at the time. Thinking of Elizabeth now, the monk sensed alarmingly a kindling fire in his groin. After several years of priesthood and the strict observance of 227 tenets, the lust had not been quenched! At an inkling of a woman, he had to subdue an awakening desire, which was unbecoming for a *piksu*. So then the *piksu* sat up and resorted to meditation.

Next morning, after breakfast, he left the temple to visit his ailing father. Napo looked deserted; its main street and lanes were empty. Jek Ching's shop remained closed since the gruesome murder of the previous headman and the henchmen. The wary shopkeeper and his family members had reason to fear the bandits since they had more wealth than most inhabitants. There had been rumours that the shopkeepers still had plenty of cash, gold ornaments and an abundant collection of antique Khmer pottery and silverware and sacred images, which desperate rice farmers severely hit by hard times had pawned.

At the Surins', Pra Prem found that Toon, his childhood love, was there, sitting silently holding her youngest child near his married sister, Piang. Poon, Kiang's wife, had been weeping, but now the presence of Pundit Piksu put a stop to her tears.

The old man, lying on the floor, turned his haggard face towards his son while Bae Charoenpol's children and Kiang Surin's boys and girls sat timidly together in a corner.

Kum unsuccessfully tried to free a few words from his parched throat. He heaved and coughed painfully. Mopping her husband's quivering lips and chin with a piece of rag, Boonliang moaned woefully: "If I could take all your pains into me to make you well again I would, old man."

Despite a lengthy priesthood, Pra Prem knew he was still linked with his people through emotions. Nevertheless, he reminded himself of a basic truth that old age, pain and death were inevitable.

For a while no one spoke. Then, in the poignant silence Piang uttered: "Have you heard that the propaganda people who left our village last night are all dead?"

"Dead? The *farang* too?" asked the priest, utterly shocked.

"Yes, all!" Toon exclaimed hoarsely; her dilated eyes glaring with the tragic flames of her sorrow.

Glancing at the tortured woman, the monk realized that his old friend had changed immeasurably. Now Toon Tinthaisong, a pitifully malnourished mother of a horde of skinny children in rags, had aged drastically, living under the fear of the Masters, the army and the police force. Of her husband, the monk recalled his first encounter of Tongdum, a native of Wa Village, when the bus from Muang dropped them at a stop from which they had to walk to Napo, Prem's last leg of the journey from London made many years ago. At the time the two men were strangers to one another, but shared the same destination. One was an indigent rice farmer on the way from town back to his wife and children; the other was the learned Luke-pi (the 'son of the goddess ghost) who had returned from abroad. Tongdum had offered to carry the heavy suitcase all the way and would not accept payment. In his mind's eye, the priest could still behold the strong limbs and the perspiration that wet the yokel's shirt, the apologetic smile for urinating by the wayside, the dogged manner of a cowered man. What was an armed struggle to the suppressed peasant who had not a chance to win?

"They were ambushed at the Fungshu Creek Crossing," Piang's voice broke into his thought.

"So near to Napo," the monk murmured.

"I'm afraid the killing will be in the village next," said Toon pointedly. "Having all these years short-changed us, cheated us with the weighing machine and beating us down when they buy from us, and for so high a price when they sell, the Chings are living in fear of the attack. If they had been honest, less mean and grabbing, they would still be able to open the shop. I realized how merciless Jek Ching could be. I was in the third year of Napo Primary School and wanted so badly to have a pencil to write on a notebook that Kroo Kumjai gave to each of us. My father did not have one *stang* on him, and a pencil cost 10 *stangs* at the time. To earn it, I searched high and low in the fields for *yaplong*, a special type of grass that horses like to eat. It took me all the morning to fill a large bamboo basket with the grass. I washed it well in a nearby pond before taking it to Jek Ching's. At the shop front I squatted by the filled basket, begging the shopkeeper to buy for his horse. If you remember, Jek Ching was the only one with a horse in our village at the time to ride to and from Muang. Spitting, and then looking at me, he agreed to part with only five *stangs*. On my knees, I begged for ten but to no avail.

Perhaps my pleading voice was not pathetic enough. Untouched and unmoved, he went inside and would not come out again, leaving me in the sun for a long while. Defiantly, I took the full basket away to the swamp and threw the grass into the water, and I went after it, pushing it out into the deepest part so that no one could collect it later."

Defiance! Pra Prem was alarmed, recalling the day when Toon was awarded the third prize at the Napo Primary School at the end of their last year there under Kroo Kumjai. *That's one side of Toon I fear would bring harm to her and her children. She shouldn't have spoken in such a tone. She does not know that for hundreds of years peasants like her all over Siam have never had any bargaining power, and she is not going to be the first to have it. Siam today is like England in the 18th century. But even in England, it had not been possible to form a pressure group until six farm workers of Tolpuddle, in Dorset, gathered under a tree in their village to go together and ask their employers not to reduce their wages of nine shillings per person per week during the hard times. One dawn, in the bitter February of 1834, the six Tolpuddle farm hands, namely George Loveless, James Loveless, James Brine, Thomas Standfield, John Standfield, and James Hammet, may their brave souls be eternally blessed, were arrested to stand trial in Dorchester for swearing an oath of unity. Such unity was feared by the ruling class, titled families and local landed gentry, that the embryonic form of a union might fan the embers of trade unionism into flames, knowing full well the extent of devastation which the French Revolution had caused. Their crime was an attempt to escape from grinding poverty and harsh employers. Their punishment was seven years of hell as convicts transported to Australia. So, my dear heart, be warned. George Loveless, a penniless English labourer, was articulate and intelligent enough to be able to make a defence statement at the trial with: "If we have violated any law, it was not done intentionally. We have injured no person or property. We were uniting to preserve ourselves, our wives and our children from utter degradation and starvation." As for you, my dear Toon, whether you're barely literate or a defenceless female or not, there won't be a chance for you and people like you to set foot in a court of law to defend yourselves. Look at several leaders of striking workers, some of whom have been killed on the spot; some disappeared without trace. So you must take great care. Don't let your vengeful fire flare visibly again.*

Meanwhile, Poon Surin covered her face with the palms of her hands and wept once more. Unknown to the monk, Kiang and

Tongdum had entered the village that night while the propaganda unit kept most of the people in the temple. They saw their wives and collected food supplies and clothes, while Panya had been hiding in the bamboo grove closest to the *gutti*, where Pra Prem had his sleeping quarters, and waited for the right moment to jet Kumjai's letter. Panya, who had won the second prize in Primary Four final examinations, whistled softly as he walked away from Wat Napo.

"Any news from Saudi?" Pra Prem asked, but did not direct the question at anyone in particular.

"A letter arrived a few days ago," said Piang. "He enclosed a draft of 500 *dollars*. As soon as we can go to a bank in Korat and get the cash, we can take Father to Nakarabury Hospital. Here is the letter. Toon has just read it."

Pundit Piksu heard fluttering wings of change when his sister uttered that foreign word, *dollars*. It sounded peculiar being spoken by his own kin, who had hardly ventured far from Napo.

Money sent from overseas meant survival. But then Toon's tragedy tore her from the roots and carried her off on a violent course. She was quite sure that Tongdum would not have left her and the children for Srisurachwood even though he had lost the land on which their hut was built to the moneylender. He and she, like most landless peasants, could have become hired labourers, working for Jek Ching and on the rice fields of other farmers around Napo. It must have been that day when an informer saw Tongdum talk to a man branded as a Communist recruiter and so assumed that Tongdum had become a Communist. Khamnan Chid and his gang stormed Toon's house early one morning and killed her father, who, in his drunken state, raised his hand to strike the intruders. The murderers would have shot her too, and perhaps her children as well, had she remained inside the hut, unseen by neighbours. Outside, while her children were clinging to her, she pleaded in vain for mercy. Shots exploded and shattered her father's skull. Having discovered several books, which were Kumjai's gifts to one of his most intelligent pupils and Kumjai's own, being kept for his return, the headman believed that he had discovered a nest of Communist propaganda.

If Tongdum had not escaped, they would have killed him on the spot. He had been repairing a chicken coop at the back of the hut when he caught a glimpse of armed men led by the headman

coming from a distance, so he crawled among the mulberry bushes and fled.

But my husband should not have taken the headman's life, Toon believed, for karma, the inevitable retribution, will eventually catch up with my father's murderers on its own course. What an awful deed Tongdum and Kiang have done; they have picked up knives and guns to avenge my father who, for merely lifting his hand, had his face blasted point-blank by the man who had paid the people to vote for him. He, who has spent so much money to buy votes, would want much more in return. After he was installed in a seat of power, he not only preyed on the inhabitants, but also learned so quickly how to use position and power for his own gain to build his power base and to enable him to run for a seat in parliament. But Tongdum and his friends should not have murdered the vile man and his hangers-on, for now the law of men will take over the force of karma. Tongdum, Kumjai, Kiang, Panya, and the rest of the bandits will be hunted and killed, and I shall never see my husband again.

Then Toon, too, wept.

Meanwhile Dekwat Luke-naam arrived. Remaining outside the hut, the temple boy called: "Venerable Brother, sir, the abbot wants you to go with Khamnan Singhon to bless the dead at the creek crossing. Khamnan is waiting for you at the Wat."

Bracing himself to face the scene of carnage, the priest hastened to follow the acolyte back to the monastery.

3

Piang Charoenpol could hardly forget the day her husband was to leave for Saudi Arabia as a worker of the Rock Moving Company, contracted to lay pipelines across the desert to the Port of Yanbu. She had laughed while he had been trying on his first pair of shoes bought in Muang. Bae's coarse and broadly spread toes would not easily yield to the mock leather, so the poor man would have to suffer blisters if he kept them on for long.

For his journey, she had prepared another set of clothes and packed them in a tote bag, while the husband had put on a clean shirt and a pair of trousers. Having thus dressed, he had looked entirely different from his former self - a windblown, sun drenched savage, who had only a loincloth to cover his nakedness.

Bae had gone to Wat Napo to say goodbye to his brother-in-law before leaving for the Celestial City, where he would take his flight to Riyadh.

Pra Prem remembered that day. The morning when he had bestowed a blessing on Bae, the monk could not help wondering how such a simple, barely literate tiller of the soil would cope with the complex international travel and with foreigners. For Bae had been plucked out of the mud and mire of an Esarn rice field, and transported into the jet-age, flying for the first time to a far-off country in search of wealth. The monk had hoped that Bae would have remained in Napo no matter how poor and hungry he had been. But the lure of money and a dream of improving the lives of family members had taken the poor man along with hundreds of others to the Middle East. So then it had not been difficult to visualize that soon, in Esarn villages, the rain-beaten, sun-struck shanties and cottages of old would have been torn down and in their place, new houses of concrete, bricks, tiles and window-panes would be standing. At that very moment, the priest had recalled Khamnan Singhon's voice: 'Electricity, television, refrigerators, electric rice cookers, electric fans, and a tar-sealed road. I promise you all these. Just go. You'll come back with your pockets full of cash.'

Not a word about the reopening of the Napo Primary School, not a word, the melancholic monk had lamented.

So then the priest had raised his voice to bless his brother-in-law: *May all calamities be averted, diseases be overcome. May you come to no harm, and then advantages and happiness be yours.*

When Bae had taken leave, the monk had followed him out of the temple to gaze at the truck, which had arrived to take several 'successful applicants' away from Napo. Prem had observed calmly the departing men. Then he had gone forward towards the edge of the village where twelve workers had been erecting a tall concrete pole. There, without being told, the lone observer had understood that shortly electricity would be had in Napo. What he had not known was that a few kilometres away another group of men, using tractors and other heavy machines, had already been at work to provide Napo with a bitumen road to Muang.

That was some months ago. Now Piang was reading Bae's letter, with a glint of hope in her eyes:

C/o Rock Moving Co.
P.O. Box 1977, Riyadh, Saudi Arabia

My dearest Piang,

In Muang we waited at the branch office of the Agency for more recruits from other villages. Eventually they arrived, truck by truck, amounting to forty-two men. Then one of the Masters put us in a ten-wheeled truck bound for Kroongtep. I was not sure whether I was actually leaving even though the thing was speeding so fast on the highway. We travelled through the night and arrived in the capital early in the morning. At the Agency's big office we were given many papers to sign. Then we were allowed to rest in a back room in which all of us sat or slept on the floor, almost on top of each other for lack of space. We also spent the night there. I am sure all of the men, like me, have wives and children at home. It is all for money that we left our loved ones behind, and for a better life when we return.

Some of the men in our group could not read or write. They had their fingers printed on the papers instead of signatures. But they have muscles and the will to do the hard work. We were taken to the airport the following day. There, in a huge hall full of people, we appeared as if we were a herd of cattle, compared to the rest of mankind that gathered there. Even then

I still could not believe that I would ever have a chance to go up in a flying machine. One of the Masters, who led us to an airline counter, said that we must not move away from the group. Even without his warning, I would not want to wander about alone there for fear of getting lost in such a huge place full of strange-looking people. I did not know from where they had come. I was becoming very nervous. Finely clothed Siamese, big built farangs and nice looking women eyed us while we clung thickly together in our dark homespun clothes. My feet started to feel the bite from the dreadful shoes.

It seemed so long before we could get into the flying machine. When it did fly, the plane seemed like a great bird trying to get itself off the ground into the air. The din it made was mortifying. I became deaf for a while, while it went up and up. Up in the skies, the clouds looked like gigantic cotton wool layers on top of one another. Eventually the flying machine went up higher than the clouds. I could not see anything below until much later. Then a river appeared like a slithering shiny snake, and houses the size of a grain of rice. At that moment the machine seemed to stop flying; it was being suspended in mid-air. The clouds far below were not moving either. At times I felt some vibration, but mostly it was smooth and we could get out of our seats to walk about. Now and then good looking young women in uniform came around and gave us food and drinks, but I could eat very little for feeling absolutely wild in the stomach.

I stopped one of these nice looking girls and asked her whether she could tell in which direction we were flying. She looked blankly at me as if she could not believe her ears that a buffalo could speak, but then she smiled sweetly.

Heaven must be still a long way off above us because when looking out of a window of the flying machine, I saw nothing but empty blue space. Below, the layers of clouds looked as if they were white skins of the earth. After so many hours of being in the air, the 'kiangbin' landed on earth at sunset. A man met us after we came out of the airport. This man looked exactly like any Siamese but strangely enough he could not speak our tongue. Later I found out that he was a Filipino. He took us out of Riyadh in two big cool vans to a camp about 300 kilometres away. Our group then broke up into units. I am now working in a rock-blasting unit, though in my life I have never handled dynamite to lay oil pipelines.

In our camp there are a number of men from Esarn. We, from Napo, are only a minority. There are a lot of Filipinos too. Our new Masters are farangs from pathet Sweden. There is a farang Master who comes to check regularly on us and talk to the Filipino foreman. I was told that his name is Rogay. One of the men, who had been here long before us, told me that Rogay is a good Master. He likes Esarn people and he has been to Siam and has an Esarn girl friend. Rogay worked together with Rosano, an Italian, who later had one of his hands cut off by the Saudi authorities because he walked out of a supermarket with goods for which he did not pay. Then Rosano was sent back to Italy.

There are bunk beds for four men to sleep in a room in our quarters. My roommates are Kumsing and Noi from Napo and Daeng from Baan Jok; each of us has a small steel cabinet to keep our belongings. The bedroom is tightly sealed to keep in the cool air that comes out from a humming machine. At the time of writing, we are to rest for a day, our day off. We cannot go anywhere around here in the desert, so I can save money to send most of it to you so you can take care of the parents and the children.

Finally, I pray to all holiness and the goodness of our parents and ancestors to protect you and everyone in our family.

With much love,

Bae

4

Having tightly tied the *krod*, a large umbrella equipped with an insect screen and a strong, sharpened wooden pole that could be pitched and set up as a tent to protect him from the sun and the rain and mosquitoes, Pundit Piksu changed his yellow robe and put on a brownish one meant for wandering. Then he left Wat Napo. His intention to wander for a week could be seen as an act of renouncing his abode, a further attempt to detach the 'self' from all possessions, whether they were *his* temple, *his* sleeping quarters or *his* mat and mosquito net. All he took with him were a begging bowl, a bottle of drinking water, a water strainer and the *krod*. However, he had a hidden motive. Going away from Napo on a rarely used route, in the opposite direction to Muang, he headed towards Srisurachwood where Kumjai and his band of bandits had taken control.

After several hours of walking on the plain, sparsely covered with tall grass and in parts by sandy soil, he came to a dried-up creek, where a few women and some of their children were digging the cracked earth, in which tiny frogs were hiding. The monk stood silently still, watching them from a bank. When the diggers became aware of his presence, they screamed and took hold of their children, fleeing from a shorn-headed man. He watched them as they sped along the barren land, marking the direction of their hamlet. Then he went down to where the women had extracted the tiny creatures from the fissures. Looking into the buckets the women had left behind, he saw *kiats* (tiny frogs) clinging to each other, being unable to jump since the captors had broken their legs. The pitiful creatures looked up at him as if to beg for mercy, and he wished that he could mend their broken legs, as he had wished to mend his crippled mind, then let them go back to relive their natural lives. But he could only pick up the buckets and place them under the scant shade of a stunted tree on the bank. At least the terrified frogs would suffer less from the searing sun until the women would return to retrieve their catch and the digging implements.

He slowly set off to follow the frightened human beings before they would vanish in the shimmering haze. After trekking for a long while, he could see some thatched roofs and lines of trees that bordered Baan Soka.

At the edge of the *moobaan* (a group of houses), he looked for a suitable place to pitch his tent. Under a tall broad-leaved *yang,* a native gum tree, he sat in the lotus position, eyes closed. He began to meditate to rid himself of hunger and thirst. After a long calm span, he opened his eyes and saw two old men sitting mindfully a few paces from him.

How long have they been sitting there, watching and waiting for the monk to come back to their world? The *piksu* cleared his throat. Calmly, he poured from the bottle some water into the palm of his left hand to rinse his parched mouth.

The moribund men then raised their hands cupped to resemble a lotus flower, and touched their bending foreheads with the tips of their fingers to perform a *namuskara* gesture. Because it was well after midday, they knew that the wandering monk could not take any victual, so they brought to him only a bowl of drinking water. They were delighted by his visit, they said, since Wat Soka had been left in ruins after the last monk departed several years ago.

"A *moobaan* without a monastery is not a good village," tremblingly said the most aged of the two. "But what can we do? Many families have moved elsewhere, and the rumours of an impending fight between the troops and the guerrillas in these parts make us sleep badly at night. We're most grateful to you for coming to give us a chance to make merit by offering you breakfast tomorrow morning and so receive your blessing." Then they left him in peace.

Alone, the priest passed the evening and the night. Within his tent, he curled round the wooden pole of the *krod,* listening to the sounds of the wild. He wondered: *How often have Kumjai, Kiang, Panya, Tongdum and the party of partisans entered Moobaan Soka at night to collect food supplies? Here, no vehicles of any kind could reach the hamlet even in dry seasons.*

Early in the morning the two doddery men returned with food, perhaps the best of what they could forage from the creek and the grassland that surrounded Soka. They offered him some sticky rice, a hard-boiled egg, and a few steamed little frogs flavoured with basil and salt. *So those women have gone back to the creek,"* the monk guessed while having his breakfast under the gaze of the two silent village elders.

When Pundit Piksu drank some water and washed his fingers, he blessed them with a mantra that began with: *Yatha wari waha pura purenti...*

A moment after the blessing had ended, one of the men enquired of his destination.

"I wish to enter Srisurachwood from the direction of Huaysai," he told them.

They appeared to be much alarmed, and beseeched him to change his course. "Please don't go into Srisurachwood. We've had so many bad tidings from that way. A number of people have fled from their villages near Srisurach. Their huts have been burnt down and many people have been killed."

"Surely no harm could come to a monk anywhere."

"Then there won't be any people to give you food, we fear."

They also feared for his life.

The priest eyed them with compassion, seeing much goodness and simplicity in them. However, in case there was an informer in Soka, the *piksu* wished it to be known that he intended to enter the woods to make contact with the fighters. "I, a monk of Wat Napo, want to talk to the outlaws to convince them to lay down arms and give themselves up to the authorities," he stated firmly.

It was difficult to read from their faces whether they could follow the holy man's speech or not, but silently the two old men bowed their greying heads to the tips of their cupped trembling hands and took leave.

Pra Prem watched them as they trudged wearily back into Soka. *News will travel quickly ahead of me, and so Kumjai and his men will be prepared and move forward towards my approach,* he was convinced. Then he undid the tent to put himself on the path towards Srisurachwood. That breakfast could be his last meal for a few days unless there were one or two more *moobaans* between Soka and the woods.

After walking a long stretch over the wasteland, the monk took to the shade of a lone ebony tree to rest. The great expanse of the Plain of Nadhone was burnt brown by the summer sun. For centuries nothing grew except some hardy gnarled trees and perennial tussocks raised in the poverty of rainless seasons.

Sitting still, in the meditating position, under the meagre shade, he visualized Kroo Kumjai trekking away from Wa Village, crossing the Plain of Napo, a lone man bearing his dreams which he wanted so much to share with the band of buffalo boys. Now, this disciple of Lord Buddha could fathom the depths of such loneliness, and progress farther to ponder on a stunted mind and an innocuous soul of a submissive and obedient child taught to learn by rote and to fear the Masters and the authorities. One could hardly blame the teachers, whether it was Kroo Kumjai or those trained teachers in Wat Borombopit Secondary School since they could hardly be aware that they had allowed themselves to become the maiming instruments. In comparison to those of the talented Europeans, his mind remained undeveloped, rendering only puerile thoughts. *Such is mine,* the monk sadly admitted. During an unguarded moment self-pity overwhelmed him, and the images of Wihelm Hagenbach, Lord Norbury, Charles Tregonning and Ian Stuart Hume, a lecturer of high calibre at the University of London, loomed over him.

Towards sunset, he approached a wooded area that had a few coconut trees, kapok trees, mango trees and bamboo groves, a sure sign of a *moobaan* on the plain. But at a closer look, he saw the burnt stilts and charred remains of huts and scorched trees. Sensing the vibes of violence and death, he stood still. Head low, the *piksu* contemplated the blackened earth.

Before it would be completely dark, he chose a spot under a seared mango tree to pitch his tent. From the bag, he brought out a tightly rolled cotton yarn that Luangpor Boon Sikune, the abbot of Wat Napo, had given him. Loosening the roll of the sacred thread, he took three steps and then let go the yarn to the ground as he walked around the *krod,* forming a perimeter of which the string had become an imaginary circular wall to protect him within.

Sitting cross-legged inside the *krod,* he calmed himself with slow, steady breathing before he would chant the *yatha* mantra to dispense compassion towards the lingering souls of men and women and children who had perished.

While the *piksu* was chanting the mantra, the wind rose into a gale and the tent shook, flapped and vibrated with a vicious force and ghostly groaning voices. Then, all ceased suddenly. Peace returned, and the cicadas resumed their humming. Nothing stirred, not even the leaves of trees for miles round. Yet he could not sleep, visualizing the scenes of atrocity and destruction, the hands that torched the shanties and pulled the triggers to kill the unarmed inhabitants.

He sensed that the *krod* had become a tiny island in the middle of a dark ocean, that he was being relentlessly watched.

He rose early. The morning came without any herald from eager roosters that once had crowed in Baan Yang. Inspecting the burnt stumps, Prem the priest guessed that there had been fourteen huts. Whoever had atrociously destroyed Baan Yang and slaughtered its people must have wanted to make sure that nothing remained to tell tales. Pity, sorrow and anger rose in his heart, but the monk held these undesirable sentiments in check, in time to reduce them to ashes.

Realising that there would not be a living soul to offer him alms, he decided to go into the woods at once. Carrying the *krod* on his left shoulder and holding the bag of the empty begging bowl with his free hand he hastened his footsteps. For a long time he progressed farther and farther, moving ahead as if he did not feel the hunger and the exhaustion and the pain caused by thorns and stones.

Time passed while the desire for food and water could still be kept at bay. He took a rest under some tall leafy trees and let the afternoon wear on. Then he trudged forward again, deeper and deeper into the forest. A long while later he heard a call. He stopped to look and listen. The woods had become dense and foreboding, and his robe had been torn at the hem by briars and twigs. His right ankle was bleeding slightly. Still he wanted to forge ahead, but the slanting sun warned him that darkness was only a short time away. In the dark the jungle could turn perilous for anyone, monks or laymen. So then while there was sunlight he looked for a level ground in a glade where he could stake the *krod*.

Looming trees towered over him; the animals of the woods watched him as he exerted his strength till the earth yielded to the sharpened wood. Then he set up the little round tent and lowered the insect screen. Turning to survey his new surroundings, he paused at one point. A moment later Srisurachwood echoed his heart-rending cry of: *Buddho! Dhammo! Sankho! Napo!* The shout sounded as if he had become incensed by sheer longing. When the echo simmered into silence, a call came from a long distance away. Was it a shriek of a wild animal in response? Returning to his tent, Pundit Piksu decided not to create the sacred parameter with the blessed cotton yarn so as to keep himself open to all forces. Thus, the fearless disciple of the Enlightened One sat down in the lotus position a pace away from the *krod*, eyes closed. Peace came softly and slowly to him in a while like a gentle caressing breeze and then exuded from him, circling the *krod* before rising upward into the canopy of nearby trees. He remained peacefully still as if he had been turned into a golden statue.

In the dusk, dark figures of twenty men and two women appeared from behind large trees and from the undergrowth. Slowly and cautiously they approached the meditating monk.

When they came closer, the leader sat down a few paces away and performed the *namuskara* to pay respect and, at the same time, set an example. The rest of the outlaws lowered themselves down on the ground, putting their weapons on one side and following suit while the priest, with his eyes still closed, remained in a trance. The disarmed men waited in silence and stillness. Some of them were convinced that they were witnessing a miracle when they imagined that they saw a golden glow surrounding the *piksu* against the falling darkness.

When Pra Prem opened his eyes, Kumjai spoke at length.

Some of the victims of thieves and injustice could not exactly follow the conversation; several of them could catch a few impressive sounds of grand words such as 'democracy', 'freedom', 'constitution', 'liberation' and 'ideologies'. But the musically gifted Panya Palaraksa did not care much for the dialogue and high mindedness. He was not even listening, as he could see himself returning to Napo and starting all over again courting a girl for marriage. He was getting tired of the war game and the life of a fugitive in a malaria-infested jungle of Esarn. But when he heard his name being called, he became alert.

"Anu, Chanticha, Panya, and the rest of you, do you trust them? Do you think they will let us walk out of Srisurach as if nothing has happened? The fact that we are still alive today is because they allow us to survive for a reason, so that they can continue to cut down trees for timber and wood chips and for land till we have no place to hide. It's the logs and the land that they want, then our lives later. As you can see, they have already had loggers and squatters in at certain parts of Srisurach just the way they have done in Kaoko, in Petchaboon. If we walk out of the forest now, we'll be walking into a trap!"

The monk could see that the former teacher of the Napo Primary School had become embittered and consumed with hatred. Yet, Prem hoped still that he could convince Kumjai and the *K-Force* men and women to follow him out of the woods and lay down their arms to the authorities next time he returned to Srisurachwood. For now they disappeared into the depths of the forest.

*These excerpts come from Pira Sudham's novel: **The Force of Karma**, The Lansdowne Edition, published in March 2002*

Design by : Cheynisa Puavong

AMARIN PRINTING AND PUBLISHING PUBLIC COMPANY LIMITED

65/16 Chaiyaphruk Road, Taling Chan, Bangkok 10170
Tel. 0 2422-9000 Fax. 0 2433-2742, 0 2434-1385
E-Mail : info@amarin.co.th **Homepage** : http://www.amarin.co.th